Katrien's DESSERT CAKES

Katrien's DESSERT CAKES

Enjoy the best of two worlds in one irresistible offering

Katrien van Zyl

PHOTOGRAPHY: JOHAN & KATRIEN VAN ZYL

METZ PRESS

Published by Metz Press
1 Cameronians Avenue
Welgemoed, 7530
South Africa

First published in 2015
This edition published in 2018

Copyright © Metz Press 2018
Copyright text © Katrien van Zyl
Photography copyright © Johan & Katrien van Zyl

All rights reserved. No part of this publication may be reproduced, stored in a retrieval system or transmitted in any form or by any means, electronic, mechanical, photocopying, recording or otherwise, without the prior written permission of the copyright owners.

Publisher	Wilsia Metz
Photographer	Johan & Katrien van Zyl
Design	Liezl Maree
Proofreader	Carla Masson
Reproduction	Robert Wong, Color Fuzion

ISBN 978-1-928376-46-0

Contents

Introduction 7
Tools and materials 8
Timing 10
Filling and coating 11

Projects

Salted caramel cake 16
Strawberries and cream cake 21
Lemon meringue cake 25
Caramel peppermint cake 28
Mock opera cake 31
Apple crumble cake 35
Almond cake 38
Chocolate mousse cake 42
Milk tart cake 46
Tiramisu cake 49
Crème brûlée cake 52
Pineapple cheesecake 56
Lime and coconut cake 60
Lemon and raspberry cake 64
Passionfruit cake 68
Apricot and coconut meringue cake 71
Hazelnut cake 74
Black Forest-inspired cake 77
Trifle cake 81
Butterscotch cake 86
Peach melba cake 90
Nougat cake 94
Chai-tea cake 98
Pavlova cake 102
Mint choc-chip cake 105

Suppliers 160
Sponsors 160

Basic cakes

Before you start baking 110
Adjusting recipes 111

Chocolate mud cake 112
Butter cake 114
Apple crumble cake 116
Coconut meringue cake 118
Chocolate fudge cake 120
Salted caramel cake 122
Malva cake 124
Almond sponge cake (*joconde*) 126

Fillings

Sugar syrup 128
Chocolate ganache filling 130
Curd filling 132
Fruit preserve filling 133
Chocolate mousse filling 135
Condensed milk custard filling 137
Traditional custard filling 139
Uncooked caramel filling 141
Lemon condensed milk filling 142

Fillings or coatings

Salted caramel ganache 143
Meringue buttercream 144
Traditional buttercream icing 146
Cream cheese icing 148

Coatings

Chocolate ganache coating 149
Chocolate glaze 151

Confectionery recipes

Meringues 153
French macarons 156

Introduction

Wizardry! With these recipes well-loved traditional tea-time and dessert favourites transmogrify into delicious gourmet cakes. Serve these cakes to your family and friends and you will see their faces light up when they taste the sweet memories of milk tart, lemon meringue or Bakewell tart or desserts such as malva pudding, trifle and apple crumble.

Cakes are usually baked for special occasions and not as an everyday treat. With this book I would like to tempt you to make scrumptious cakes with gourmet flavours for everyday dessert or even for afternoon tea. I hope that this book will inspire you to play with different flavour combinations to create your own dessert cakes. The cake, filling and coating recipes can be mixed and matched to create a unique taste sensation every time you bake and decorate a cake.

Some of the cakes have been lavishly decorated and can be used for special occasions but the idea behind these cakes is more about the delectable taste than the decorative effect. You do not have to feel daunted by the different components that make up each cake; they can be made days or weeks in advance and kept refrigerated or frozen to give you plenty of time to assemble. Whether you want to make and assemble the cake in one day or whether you work full time and can only do a little each day, there are clear instructions and tips to help you create the cake in your own time. Of coarse you can also buy ready-made cakes and cupcakes and fill them with any of the delicious fillings in the last section of the book.

Featured here are 25 dessert cake projects from start to finish, showing you step by step how to create your own mouth-watering desserts. I have also included accompanying cupcakes for each cake in case you prefer a mini version of these cakes served in individual portions.

At the beginning of the book it is clearly explained how to fill, cover and prepare the cake and at the back of the book are tried and trusted recipes for cakes, fillings, coatings and more, including guides for increasing the recipes to suit your needs.

Enjoy creating your dessert!

Katrien

www.katrienscakes.co.za

Tools and materials

Cake boards, cake cards or cardboards

Cake boards, cake cards or sturdy cardboards are used to carry cakes. To make your own cake board, place a cake tin of the same size used to bake the cake on a piece of cardboard. Draw the shape around the cake tin to the same size or 5 mm ($1/5$ in) wider than the cake. Cut out the cardboard and cover it with clingfilm (plastic wrap) or foil. Secure the clingfilm or foil with adhesive tape.

Cooking or baking chocolate

I have mostly used this type of chocolate or a mixture of $1/3$ eating chocolate to $2/3$ cooking or baking chocolate in the recipes at the back of this book and to make decorative items for my cakes. Melt the chopped chocolate in a microwave oven at 20% power or on the defrost setting at 30-second intervals until the chocolate is almost fully melted but with a few chunky pieces still visible. Stir the chocolate until it is fully melted.

Food colouring

Liquid food colouring can be bought at any supermarket and is usually available in pink, red, blue, yellow and green. Liquid food colouring is water based and can be used to colour cake batter, buttercream or ganache coating. To colour chocolate with liquid food colouring, mix 2-10 drops of liquid food colouring with 1.25-2.5 ml ($1/4$-$1/2$ t) vegetable oil at a time. Gel (paste) food colouring can be bought at baking supply shops and is available in many colours. It is the easiest colouring to work with as it does not affect the texture of cakes, buttercream, ganache or chocolate too much and can be added directly to these items.

Palette knife or spatula

Used to apply icing or ganache to the cake. Dip your palette knife or spatula into hot water and glide it over your buttercream or ganache to smooth the surface or use it to spread melted chocolate onto non-stick baking paper.

Piping bags

Bags can be made from non-stick baking paper, tracing paper or cellophane. You can also use zip-lock bags or disposable plastic piping bags to pipe icing.

Piping nozzles

Made especially for cake decorating, these piping nozzles are used to pipe perfectly round macaroons or meringues or to pipe buttercream or ganache onto the cake.

Plastic or metal scrapers

Used for evenly applying buttercream icing or ganache to the outside of cakes. They can also be used to thinly spread chocolate onto your work surface. Differently sized metal scrapers can be bought at any hardware shop.

Timing

This suggested schedule is included to help you plan your dessert cakes in advance and give you peace of mind knowing the cake will be finished on time for dessert or for a special occasion. I try to complete a little each day rather than everything at once but if you have the time, you could bake the cake, make the filling and coating and assemble the cake in one day.

Up to 2 weeks in advance

- Make any decorations that can be stored in an airtight container, such as chocolate decorations, candied or spiced nuts and paper collars.
- If preferred, make and freeze the fillings, coatings and cake layers until required.
- See the recipe section at the back of the book for wonderful ideas for cakes and fillings.

2 Days in advance

- Bake the cake layers and leave in the tins to cool.
- If you have previously frozen the cake layers or filling or coating, put them in the refrigerator to thaw overnight.

1 Day in advance

- Make your filling and coating.
- If you have thawed the cake layers in the refrigerator, take them out to come to almost room temperature. They should remain slightly chilled.
- Fill the cake layers. If you have used perishable fillings such as fruit fillings, custard or cheese-based icings, keep your filled cake in an airtight container in the refrigerator.
- Make any decorations that can be made a day in advance.

On the day

- Make any decorations that can only be made a few hours in advance, such as toffee apples.
- Coat the cake with ganache or buttercream and decorate it.
- If you have placed the cake in a refrigerator, take it out at least 30 minutes to 1 hour in advance to serve at room temperature.
- Eat and enjoy!

To bake and decorate the cake in one day, put the cake layers in a freezer for 30 minutes to cool quickly. Pour the cake filling and coating into baking trays (sheets) and put in the refrigerator to cool down quickly before use.

Filling and coating

Filling and coating guide

Round cake	15 cm (6 in)	17.5 cm (7 in)	20 cm (8 in)	22 cm (9 in)	25 cm (10 in)	30 cm (12 in)
Square cake	12 cm (5 in)	15 cm (6 in)	17.5 cm (7 in)	20 cm (8 in)	22 cm (9 in)	28 cm (11 in)
Filling amount	375 ml 1½ cups 13½ fl oz	500 ml 2 cups 18 fl oz	750 ml 3 cups 27 fl oz	875 ml 3½ cups 31½ fl oz	1 000 ml 4 cups 36 fl oz	1 500 ml 6 cups 54 fl oz
Buttercream or ganache coating to create a thick circle	125 ml ½ cup 4½ fl oz	180 ml ¾ cup 6¾ fl oz	250 ml 1 cup 9 fl oz	310 ml 1¼ cups 11¼ fl oz	375 ml 1½ cups 14 fl oz	500 ml 2 cups 18 fl oz
Coating amount	375 ml 1½ cups 13½ fl oz	500 ml 2 cups 18 fl oz	750 ml 3 cups 27 fl oz	875 ml 3½ cups 31½ fl oz	1 000 ml 4 cups 36 fl oz	1 500 ml 6 cups 54 fl oz

Most of the flavour and texture for your dessert cake is in the filling. The cake layers serve as a vehicle to carry your fillings.

> **Note:** The cakes in this book are usually baked in two baking tins, yielding two layers each about 4-5 cm (1²⁄₃-2 in) high. Each layer can be sliced and filled with ganache, buttercream, mousse, fruit preserve or custard, yielding four layers which, when placed on top of one another, form a whole cake approximately 10 cm (4 in) high.

I prefer to bake the cake layers a day in advance so that they can firm up. The baked cake layers can be left in their tins overnight and then divided, filled and coated the next day. However, if you are pressed for time, let the cake layers cool in the tin for 15 minutes after baking and then put the tins with the cakes in the freezer for 30 minutes. This will cool and firm the cake quickly so that you can fill and coat it immediately.

Filling

- ✓ 2 cake layers each about 4-5 cm (1²/₃-2 in) high
- ✓ 1 cake board, cake card or cardboard covered with clingfilm or foil of the same diameter as the cake, or a serving plate or cake stand
- ✓ filling such as traditional buttercream, meringue buttercream, fruit preserve, custard or mousse (see table on p 11 to determine quantity)

1. Flip the cake tins over to let the cakes fall out and remove the non-stick baking paper from the cakes.
2. If the tops of the cakes look uneven, cut them even with a long serrated knife.
3. Divide each cake into two layers by cutting it in half horizontally with a long serrated knife or cake cutting wire. Keep the knife or cutting wire steady with one hand while moving the cake around with the other hand.

4. Slide a large egg lifter in between the two cut layers of each cake so that the top layer is resting on the egg lifter and set it aside. You will now have 4 cake layers. Keep one of the bottom layers to use as the top of your filled cake tier; if you turn it upside down it will be flat and smooth where the non-stick baking paper was attached.

5. Put a dollop of filling mixture, buttercream or ganache on the cake board, cake card or clingfilm- or foil-covered cardboard and spread it thinly to cover the whole board.
6. Place one cake layer onto the cake board, cake card or cardboard or directly on a serving plate or cake stand.

7. Using the guide above, divide the required amount of filling into three or however many layers you need to fill. Spoon the filling onto the centre of a cake layer and spread it towards the outside edge with a palette knife.
8. If you are using a thin filling such as custard or fruit preserve, you have to create a dam around the outside edge of the cake layer. Thicken some of your buttercream coating by adding more icing (confectioner's) sugar until it feels very stiff, or use ganache coating. Put the stiffened buttercream or ganache coating in a zip-lock or disposable piping bag and snip off the tip. Pipe a thick circle of about 1 cm (½ in) along the edge to create a wall for the filling.
9. Pour or spoon the filling onto the cake layer making sure that the filling is level with the buttercream or ganache circle.

10. Place another layer of cake on top of the first and repeat the filling process. Layer and fill until the whole cake has been stacked, placing the bottom layer you kept aside on top of the stacked cake.
11. The filled cake can be frozen for use at a later date or left in the refrigerator overnight. This will give you a firmer cake to decorate, but let the cake come to room temperature before coating. If you are pressed for time, coat the cake directly after filling.

Coating with buttercream or ganache

If you have frozen your filled cake beforehand, be sure to defrost it thoroughly and let it come to room temperature before coating or decorating.

- ✓ 1 filled cake on a cake board, cake card or cardboard of the same diameter as the cake or on a serving plate or cake stand
- ✓ traditional buttercream, meringue buttercream or ganache coating (see the recipe section at the back of the book for coating ideas)

1. Place the cake on its board on a large cutting board (or a cake turntable) to make it easier to coat. If preferred, place non-slip fabric or double-sided adhesive tape underneath the cake board so that the cake cannot move around.
2. If the cake is placed on a board of exactly the same size as the cake, cut about 5 mm (1/5 in) off the sides of the cake so that the whole cake is slightly smaller than the board. This will make room to spread your coating.
3. Take about 1/3 of the buttercream or ganache coating and spread the outside of the cake with a thin layer using your palette knife or spatula to crumb coat (dirty ice) the cake. If using ganache coating, soften it in a microwave oven at 20% power or on the defrost setting, stirring at 30-second intervals until the ganache is very soft.
4. If it is a hot day, put the cake in a refrigerator for 15 minutes for the icing or ganache to set.
5. Use buttercream at room temperature or put the leftover ganache in a microwave oven at 20% power or on the defrost setting and stir at 30-second intervals until the ganache has the consistency of smooth peanut butter.

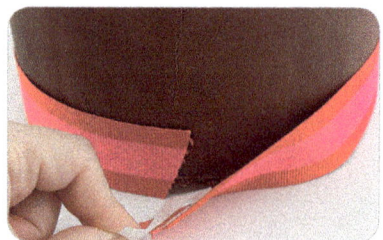

6. Scoop buttercream or ganache onto the sides of the cake and roughly spread it with your palette knife or spatula, flattening any buttercream or ganache protruding over the top of the cake.
7. Spread more buttercream or ganache on top of the cake and either leave it with a rough finish or follow the rest of the steps.
8. If you want a very neat finish on the cake, smooth the icing or ganache on the cake by placing your palette knife, a long ruler or a scraper against the side of the cake and scrape the icing or ganache towards you. Start all the way at the back of the cake and scrape the buttercream or ganache towards you with the one hand while turning the cutting board with the other.
9. Scrape any excess buttercream or ganache back into the bowl and periodically clean the palette knife, ruler or scraper with a damp cloth.
10. Repeat spreading dollops of buttercream or ganache on top of the cake and flattening it with your palette knife or spatula. Scrape the top of the cake with your palette knife, a long ruler or a scraper, from the outside edge towards the centre, trying to keep it as level as possible. Scrape any excess buttercream or ganache back into the bowl.
11. If you see any uneven spots or ridges on the cake you can use a clean finger to wipe over the area or use a sharp knife dipped into boiled water and dried on a clean cloth to cut off any unwanted ridges or bumps.
12. If the icing still does not look smooth enough, put the cake in the freezer for 15 minutes or in a refrigerator for 30 minutes. Then dip your palette knife or spatula into boiled water and let any excess water drip off or wipe it with a clean cloth. Spread the coating into a smooth layer around the cake and on top of the cake.
13. Use an egg lifter to lift the cake and its board off the cutting board. Slide your other hand underneath and place the iced cake on a cake stand or serving platter by sliding it off the egg lifter.
14. There will be some buttercream or ganache left over after scraping the cake to get a smooth coating. Freeze the leftover coating for use on another cake.
15. You might like to decorate the cake with a ribbon. Cut a piece of ribbon 2.5 cm (1 in) longer than the circumference of the cake. Cut a 2.5 cm (1 in) piece of double-sided adhesive tape and stick it onto one end of the ribbon. Fasten the ribbon around the cake, ensuring that the adhesive tape is on the inside of the ribbon overlapping the other end.

Tip

You can freeze your coated cake. Cover the cake with plastic clingfilm and put in a freezer for up to three months. To thaw the cake, refrigerate it overnight and take it out of the refrigerator 30 minutes to 1 hour before serving.

Projects

Salted caramel cake

Decadently sweet layers of cooked caramel custard fill this dessert cake. Coarse ground sea salt is added to cut through the sweetness and almond brittle sprinkle is used as decoration.

Makes 12-16 slices

Almond brittle

This is a sweet and crunchy almond brittle and totally addictive. Spread the brittle with melted chocolate while it is still warm for an even more decadent treat. Makes 1 tray of almond brittle pieces or 290 g (10¼ oz).

- ✓ 50 g (½ cup/1¾ oz) flaked or slivered almonds
- ✓ a large pinch of course ground sea salt or Maldon salt
- ✓ 115 g (½ cup/4 oz) salted butter or baking margarine
- ✓ 125 g (²⁄₃ cup/4½ oz) white sugar
- ✓ 15 ml (1 T) liquid glucose or golden syrup (light corn syrup) (buy glucose at your pharmacy)
- ✓ 15 ml (1 T) water

Tip

Use any nuts of your choice instead of the flaked almonds. Almond brittle will keep for a week in an airtight container at room temperature placed in single layers on non-stick baking paper.

1. Put the almonds in a microwave-safe bowl and heat at full power stirring at 30-second intervals until the almonds are lightly browned. Add the salt.
2. Line a baking tray (sheet) with non-stick baking paper and spray with non-stick cooking spray. Set another piece of non-stick baking paper aside.
3. In a non-stick saucepan, combine butter, sugar, liquid glucose or golden syrup and water. Cook over medium high heat, stirring constantly, until the mixture boils. Boil without stirring to hard crack stage or 150 °C (300 °F) on a sugar thermometer or until the mixture has a dark brown caramel colour.
4. Remove from the heat and working quickly, stir in the toasted almonds and salt and pour the mixture into the lined baking tray.
5. Place the second piece of non-stick baking paper on top of the almond mixture and roll it into a thin layer with a rolling pin. If you prefer, spread the mixture with a non-stick spatula.
6. When the almond brittle has cooled, break it into uneven shards.

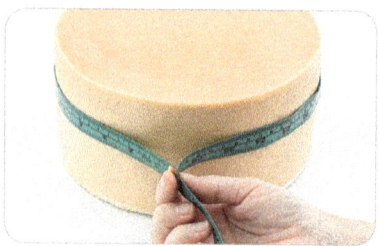

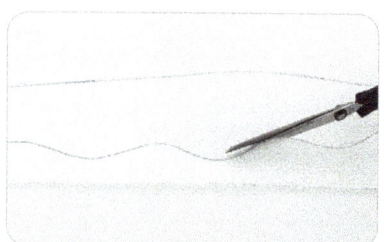

Decorative cake border

✓ The almond sprinkle used in the decorative cake border is made from almond brittle. Crush a portion of 90 g (½ cup/3¼ oz) into small pieces with a food processor. If you do not have a food processor, put the almond brittle in a bag and smash it with a hammer or a meat mallet.
✓ Keep the rest of the brittle whole to decorate the cake.
✓ Cut out any pattern from non-stick baking paper and use it to create a decorative pattern around the cake. Of course you could also use any edible items such as flaked almonds, chocolate vermicelli (sprinkles), nonpareils (hundreds-and-thousands), chopped nuts, praline, peanut brittle, chocolate shavings, cake crumbs or cookie crumbs.

Your cake should be coated with a final layer of coating before starting with this technique.

1. Make a template for the decorative pattern by determining the exact size of collar you need to cover the cake:
   – Measure the height of the cake;
   – Measure the circumference of the cake;
   – Cut a piece of non-stick baking paper to this size.
2. Draw any pattern such as a wave anywhere on the paper and cut it out with scissors or use scrapbook scissors to cut out a pattern. Spray non-stick cooking spray on the side of the paper template which will be against the cake.

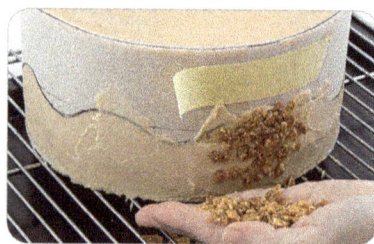

3. Place your coated cake on a cooling rack with a baking tray (sheet) underneath to catch any sprinkle that might fall off.
4. Fold the paper template around the cake, either around the top or bottom edge as you prefer. Stick the ends together with adhesive tape.
5. If the coating on the cake has set firmly, spread leftover coating on the open areas or brush on apricot jam or sugar syrup for the decorations to adhere to.

6. Spoon some of the almond brittle sprinkle into your hand and press it against the open areas at the sides of the cake. Repeat until all the open areas have been covered.
7. Loosen the adhesive tape and remove the paper from the cake to reveal the wavy pattern. If the paper sticks to the coating, put the cake in a refrigerator for 30 minutes or in a freezer for 15 minutes for the coating to set before removing the paper.
8. Use any remaining almond brittle on top of the cake or for another project.

Make the complete cake

- ✓ 2 round 20 cm (8 in) layers of the salted caramel cake (p. 122)
- ✓ 1 round 20 cm (8 in) cake board or cardboard wrapped in foil or clingfilm
- ✓ 1 round serving plate or cake stand
- ✓ 1 batch condensed milk custard filling: caramel variation (p. 138)
- ✓ coarse ground sea salt or Maldon salt
- ✓ 1 batch caramel sauce

Caramel sauce

- ✓ 45 g (¼ cup/1½ oz) brown treacle sugar or demerara sugar
- ✓ 150 g (½ cup/5 oz) golden syrup
- ✓ 60 g (¼ cup/2 oz) salted butter or baking margarine
- ✓ 125 ml (½ cup) cream

1. Stir together the sugar, syrup and butter in a saucepan on the stove at medium heat.
2. Once the sugar has dissolved, bring to a light boil. Let it boil for about 2 minutes.
3. Add the cream and boil for another 2 minutes, stirring constantly.
4. Remove from the heat and refrigerate the sauce until cool.
5. Keep 60 ml (¼ cup/2¼ fl oz) of the caramel sauce separate to use on top of the cake for decoration. The rest of the sauce will be poured onto each layer over the filling.

- ✓ 1 batch salted caramel ganache coating (p. 143) or caramel meringue buttercream (p. 145) or caramel traditional buttercream (p. 147)
- ✓ decorative cake border made with 1 batch almond brittle with 90 g (½ cup/3¼ oz) crushed and the rest kept whole to decorate the top of the cake as described above
- ✓ gold dragees (optional)

Assembling and decorating the cake

1. Divide the cake layers and place the bottom cake layer on the board.
2. Fill each layer with 250 ml (1 cup/9 fl oz) of the caramel custard filling. Pour 60 ml (¼ cup/2¼ fl oz) of the caramel sauce over each layer of filling and sprinkle a pinch or two of the salt over the filling before you stack the next one.

3. Coat the cake with the caramel-flavoured coating. (See filling and coating cakes p. 11.)
4. Decorate the cake with a decorative border as described above and place the cake on a serving plate or cake stand.
5. The caramel custard is perishable; therefore keep the cake refrigerated in an airtight container until 1 hour before serving.
6. Pour the reserved caramel sauce on top of the cake and arrange almond brittle shards haphazardly on top of the cake. Sprinkle leftover crushed almond brittle and optional gold dragees on the cake.

Note: If you can wait that long, this cake tastes even better after being refrigerated for 1-2 days. The caramel sauce is absorbed into the cake layers and the caramel flavour deepens.

Quick and easy version

Use store-bought peanut brittle instead of homemade almond brittle.

Cupcakes

1. Bake salted caramel cupcakes (p. 123).
2. Spoon or pipe caramel condensed milk custard filling onto each cupcake.
3. Pour caramel sauce over the caramel custard and sprinkle with a pinch of coarse ground sea salt or Maldon salt.
4. Decorate with almond brittle.

Strawberries and cream cake

Light layers of strawberry mousse combine with strawberry cake to make this luscious treat. Here a chocolate ruffle flower is used as decoration but fresh strawberries could also complete it.

Makes 8-12 slices

Chocolate ruffle flower

Making ruffle flowers is a difficult technique to master. If you have not worked with chocolate before, rather make the chocolate curls on p. 49 or decorate the top of the cake with strawberries.

✓ The chocolate ruffles are made with 200 g (7 oz) white chocolate.

To melt your chocolate

Melt the chopped chocolate in a microwave oven at 20% power or on the defrost setting at 30-second intervals until the chocolate is almost fully melted but with a few chunky pieces still visible. Stir the chocolate until it is fully melted. Add 5-10 ml (1-2 t) vegetable oil to the chocolate to make it more pliable and to have it set more slowly. Melt only a ¼ of the chocolate at a time or melt it as required.

1. Line a baking tray (sheet) with non-stick baking paper.
2. Heat your work surface slightly by blowing hot air over it with a hairdryer.
3. Pour about a ¼ of the melted chocolate onto your work surface (a marble slab, flat tile, thick rectangular glass plate, stainless steel counter or granite worktop). You can put your marble slab, tile or glass plate in the refrigerator beforehand for 10 minutes to speed up the cooling of the chocolate if it is a very hot day.
4. Scrape the chocolate with a dough or metal scraper or palette knife until it has cooled slightly and then spread it flat into a very thin layer.
5. Quickly clean the excess chocolate off the scraper or palette knife with a sharp knife.
6. Hold a palette knife flat and parallel to the surface of the worktop and scrape or slice the chocolate from the worktop towards you in a semi-circle while simultaneously pinching one side of the ruffle on the palette knife with your other hand. Work in one even, fast motion so that a big ruffle forms.
7. Your palette knife should be almost flat on the work surface and the blade can even bend slightly. If your palette knife is at an angle a roll will form instead of a ruffle. If the chocolate is still too soft it will bunch up on the palette knife instead of making a ruffle and if the chocolate has set too hard it

will make splinters instead of a ruffle. Keep a dry cloth handy to clean the palette knife in between making ruffles.

8. Scrape the leftover chocolate off your work surface to re-melt for making more ruffles.
9. Place the finished ruffles on the baking tray to cool and harden. You could put the tray in the refrigerator for 10 minutes to cool the ruffles more quickly.
10. Place a piece of non-stick baking paper on a side plate and pour some of the leftover chocolate in the centre of the paper.
11. Place ruffles in a circle on the outside edge of the side plate on top of the melted chocolate.
12. Place more ruffles in the centre, on top of the previous row of ruffles and attach them with more melted chocolate. Continue placing ruffles in a circle and in the centre of the flower until you are satisfied with the appearance.
13. Put the side plate with the flower in a refrigerator for 10 minutes to set.
14. Remove the paper from the bottom of the flower and place the flower on top of the cake. Decorate the centre of the flower with a freshly chopped strawberry.

Tip

The chocolate ruffle flower can be made up to two weeks in advance and stored in an airtight container in a cool dark cupboard.

Make the complete cake

- ✓ 2 round 15 cm (6 in) layers of butter cake: strawberry variation (p. 114)
- ✓ 1 round 15 cm (6 in) cake board or cardboard wrapped in foil or clingfilm
- ✓ 1 round serving plate or cake stand
- ✓ 45 ml (3 T) strawberry-flavoured sugar syrup (p. 129)
- ✓ ½ batch chocolate mousse: strawberry variation made from:
    - ½ batch chocolate mousse filling (p. 135) made with white chocolate
    - ¼ batch strawberry fruit preserve (p. 133) or 30 ml (2 T) strawberry jam
- ✓ ⅔ batch milk chocolate ganache coating (p. 149) or chocolate meringue buttercream (p. 145) or chocolate traditional buttercream (p. 147)
- ✓ chocolate ruffle flower made with 200 g (7 oz) white chocolate
- ✓ fresh strawberries (optional)
- ✓ ribbon 55 cm (22 in) and double-sided adhesive tape (optional)

Assembling and decorating the cake

1. Divide the cake layers and place the bottom cake layer on the board.
2. Brush each layer with the strawberry sugar syrup before you fill it and stack the next one.

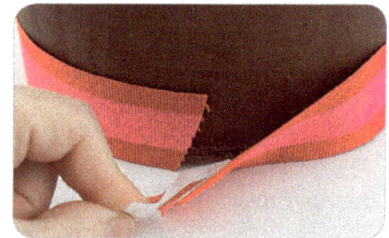

3. Pipe a circle around the edge of each cake layer with the milk chocolate ganache coating or chocolate buttercream to create a barrier for the light mousse. Use 125 ml (½ cup/4½ fl oz) in total for all three layers.
4. Fill each circle with 125 ml (½ cup/4½ fl oz) of the strawberry chocolate mousse filling.
5. Coat the cake with the rest of the chocolate-flavoured coating. (See filling and coating cakes p. 11.)
6. Spoon a dollop of the coating on top of the cake to attach the ruffle flower.
7. Place the flower on the cake and place a teaspoonful of freshly chopped strawberries in the centre of the flower.
8. If preferred, fasten a 55 cm (22 in) ribbon around the bottom of the cake and attach the ends with double-sided adhesive tape.
9. The strawberry chocolate mousse is perishable; therefore keep the cake refrigerated in an airtight container until 1 hour before serving.
10. Place the cake on a serving plate or cake stand to serve.

Tip

You could replace the strawberry mousse with strawberry-flavoured white chocolate ganache filling. Make ½ a batch of ganache filling (p. 130) using white chocolate and mix in a ¼ batch of strawberry fruit preserve (p. 133) or 30 ml (2 T) strawberry jam.

Quick and easy version

Replace the chocolate ruffle flower with freshly sliced strawberries.

Cupcakes

1. Bake cupcakes using the strawberry butter cake (p. 115).
2. Cut a small hole into the top of each cupcake using an apple corer or a knife.
3. Brush each cupcake with strawberry sugar syrup.
4. Spoon or pipe strawberry chocolate mousse filling into each hole.
5. Spread the top of each cupcake with milk chocolate ganache coating or chocolate buttercream.
6. Place a teaspoonful of strawberry mousse on top of the ganache.
7. Decorate with a chocolate ruffle or chocolate curls (see p. 49) and freshly sliced strawberries.

Lemon meringue cake

The tartness of lemon and the sweetness of condensed milk are perfect companions in this mouth-watering dessert cake and bring back sweet childhood memories. As a topping, use homemade or purchased meringues.

Makes 12-16 slices

Paper collar

Placing a pretty patterned paper collar around the cake gives it a new dimension and can make the cake even more special for a birthday or special occasion dessert.

- paper collar made from a strip of scrapbook paper, gift wrap or handmade paper – for a 20 cm (8 in) cake it will be about 7.5 cm (3 in) wide and 70 cm (28 in) long
- wax paper
- double-sided tape
- ribbon 65 cm (26 in) (optional)

1. To prepare the paper collar for the cake:
   - Measure the height of the cake and subtract ¼ of the measurement;
   - Measure the circumference of the cake and add 5 cm (2 in) to the circumference.
2. Cut your chosen paper to this size. You could also use scrapbook scissors to give your paper collar a patterned edge.
3. To protect the cake and prevent any chemicals on the paper from transferring to the cake, cut a piece of wax paper 5 mm ($1/5$ in) smaller than the paper collar.
4. Attach double-sided adhesive tape to the inside of the paper collar and stick the wax paper to it, ensuring that the waxy side will be placed against the cake.
5. Place the collar around the cake, attaching the overlapping ends of the paper with double-sided adhesive tape.
6. If preferred, fasten a ribbon around the collar.

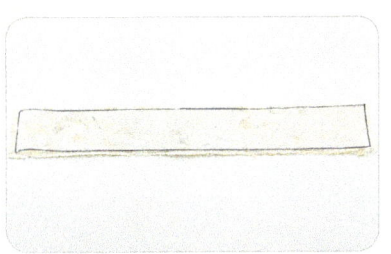

Make the complete cake

- 2 round 20 cm (8 in) layers of butter cake: lemon variation (p. 115) or chocolate mud cake: lemon variation (p. 113)
- 1 round 20 cm (8 in) cake board or cardboard wrapped in foil or clingfilm
- 1 round serving plate or cake stand
- 1 batch lemon condensed milk filling (p. 142)
- 1 1/3 batch chocolate ganache coating (p. 149) using white chocolate or 1 1/3 batch meringue buttercream (p. 144) or traditional buttercream (p. 146)
- paper collar (ribbon optional)
- 1 batch marbled spiky meringues (p. 153) using yellow and orange food colouring

Assembling and decorating the cake

1. Divide the cake layers and place the bottom cake layer on the board. Fill each layer before stacking the next on top.
2. Pipe a circle around the edge of the cake layer with white chocolate ganache coating or buttercream, using 250 ml (1 cup/9 fl oz) in total for all three layers.
3. Fill each circle with 250 ml (1 cup/9 fl oz) of the lemon condensed milk filling.
4. Coat the cake with the rest of the coating. (See filling and coating cakes p. 11.)
5. The lemon condensed milk filling is perishable; therefore keep the cake refrigerated in an airtight container until 1 hour before serving.
6. To serve, place the cake on a serving plate or cake stand.
7. Place the paper collar around the cake (see p. 25).
8. Top the cake with marbled spiky meringues.

Quick and easy version

Use a store-bought cake or use store-bought meringues to decorate the cake.

Cupcakes

1. Bake lemon butter (p. 115) or lemon chocolate mud (p. 113) cupcakes.
2. Cut a small hole into the top of each cupcake using an apple corer or a knife.
3. Spoon or pipe lemon condensed milk filling into each cupcake.
4. Spread the top with white chocolate ganache coating or buttercream.
5. Decorate with a meringue.

Caramel peppermint cake

This dessert cake is filled with delectable layers of caramel filling and peppermint chocolate and topped with chocolate shards.

Makes 12-16 slices

Chocolate shards

- 75 g (2²⁄₃ oz) peppermint chocolate or ½ a slab of Nestlé Peppermint Crisp™ or Nestlé Peppermint Aero™
- 200 g (7 oz) white chocolate

1. Cut a piece of non-stick baking paper big enough to fit onto a baking tray (sheet). Turn the tray upside down. Secure the paper onto the tray with adhesive tape. If it is a cold day, heat the underside of the baking tray by blowing hot air onto it with a hairdryer.
2. Chop the peppermint chocolate into small pieces or grate it with a coarse grater. Set aside.
3. Melt the white chocolate in a microwave oven at 20% power or on the defrost setting at 30-second intervals until the chocolate is almost fully melted but with a few chunky pieces still visible. Remove and stir the chocolate until it is fully melted.
4. Pour the melted chocolate in a thick line onto the non-stick baking paper on the tray.
5. Using a palette knife, quickly spread the chocolate into a thin layer on the baking paper.
6. Before the chocolate sets, sprinkle the chopped or grated peppermint chocolate all over the surface of the white chocolate.
7. Put the tray with chocolate in the refrigerator for no longer than 10 minutes, to let the chocolate cool and set completely.
8. Remove the chocolate from the refrigerator and lift it off the paper. Carefully break or snap off big pieces to make your shards.

Tip

The chocolate shards can be made up to two weeks in advance and stored in an airtight container in a cool dark cupboard.

Make the complete cake

- ✓ 2 round 20 cm (8 in) layers of the chocolate fudge cake (p. 120) or mud cake: dark chocolate variation (p. 113)
- ✓ 1 round 20 cm (8 in) cake board or cardboard wrapped in foil or clingfilm
- ✓ 1 round serving plate or cake stand
- ✓ 60 ml (¼ cup/2¼ fl oz) mint-flavoured sugar syrup (p. 129) or liqueur
- ✓ 1 batch uncooked caramel filling (p. 141)
- ✓ 75 g (2⅔ oz) Grated peppermint chocolate or ½ of a 150 g (5¼ oz) slab of Nestlé Peppermint Crisp™ or Nestlé Peppermint Aero™
- ✓ 1 Batch salted caramel ganache coating (p. 143) or caramel meringue buttercream (p. 145) or caramel traditional buttercream (p. 147)
- ✓ Chocolate shards made with 75 g (2⅔ oz) peppermint chocolate and 200 g (7 oz) white chocolate
- ✓ Fresh mint leaves (optional)

Assembling and decorating the cake

1. Divide the cake layers and place the bottom cake layer on the board.
2. Brush each cake layer with mint sugar syrup or peppermint liqueur before filling and stacking the next one.
3. Stir the caramel filling to soften it. Cover each cake layer with 250 ml (1 cup/9 fl oz) of the filling and sprinkle with 2 tablespoons of grated peppermint chocolate.
4. Coat the cake with the caramel-flavoured coating. (See filling and coating cakes p. 11.)
5. Place the cake on a serving plate or cake stand.
6. Dab some leftover ganache or buttercream on the back of each chocolate shard and press them at random against the side of the cake.
7. Arrange the remaining chocolate shards and grated peppermint chocolate on top of the cake. Decorate the cake with optional fresh mint leaves.
8. The uncooked caramel filling is perishable; therefore keep the cake refrigerated in an airtight container until 1 hour before serving.

Cupcakes

1. Bake cupcakes using the recipes for chocolate fudge cake (p. 120) or caramel butter cake (p. 115).
2. Brush each cupcake with mint sugar syrup.
3. Spoon or pipe uncooked caramel filling onto each cupcake.
4. Decorate with chocolate shards or grated peppermint chocolate.

Mock opera cake

This is a simplified version of the traditional opera gâteau, usually made with thin layers of almond sponge (*joconde*) cake. It is layered with coffee buttercream and milk chocolate ganache and decorated with a shiny chocolate glaze.

Makes 12-16 slices

Patterned glaze

Your cake should be filled, coated, chilled and ready to be decorated before proceeding with these steps.

- ✓ 1 batch dark chocolate glaze (p. 151) – half the recipe or 250 ml (1 cup/9 fl oz) will cover the cake but make the full amount to have enough glaze to pour
- ✓ 60 g (2 oz) white chocolate
- ✓ 5 ml (1 t) vegetable oil
- ✓ a drop of blue gel food colouring or 3 drops of blue liquid food colouring

Note: If you are unsure about colouring chocolate, rather use plain melted white chocolate and melted milk chocolate to contrast with the dark glaze.

1. Prepare the dark chocolate glaze and leave the mixture at room temperature or in the refrigerator to thicken.
2. If the mixture has set and is too firm to pour, reheat it in a microwave oven at 20% power or on the defrost setting until it is just above body temperature or runny enough to pour over the cake. It should have the consistency of thin custard. Be careful not to overheat the glaze as it could melt the coating on the cake. Stir gently so that you do not incorporate too many air bubbles into the glaze.
3. Place the slightly chilled coated cake on a cooling rack over a baking tray (sheet) and pour the glaze over the cake preferably through a sieve, covering all the sides and moving the sieve and glaze towards the centre of the cake to cover the top.
4. If you see any air bubbles, quickly burst them with a sterilized pin or toothpick.
5. Melt the white chocolate and add 5 ml (1 t) vegetable oil to make the chocolate set more slowly.
6. Colour half of the chocolate with blue food colouring.
7. Use teaspoons to pour the white chocolate and blue chocolate individually over the cake in a swirling and flicking motion.

8. Scrape the leftover glaze from the baking tray back into a container to reuse for another cake.
9. Carefully lift the cake from the cooling rack with an egg lifter, placing your other hand underneath the cake board, and slide the cake onto a serving plate or cake stand with the egg lifter. Put the cake in the refrigerator for 20-30 minutes for the glaze to set.

Tip

The chocolate glaze can be refrigerated in an airtight container for up to one month or frozen for six months. Bring back to room temperature before use.

Make the complete cake

- ✓ 2 round 20 cm (8 in) layers of butter cake: almond variation (p. 115) – for a special treat, bake thin layers of almond sponge (joconde) (p. 126)
- ✓ 1 round 20 cm (8 in) cake board or cardboard wrapped in foil or clingfilm
- ✓ 1 round serving plate or cake stand
- ✓ 125 ml (½ cup/4½ fl oz) Coffee-flavoured sugar syrup (p. 129) or Kahlua liqueur
- ✓ ½ batch milk chocolate ganache filling (p. 130)
- ✓ 1½ batches of coffee meringue buttercream (p. 144) or coffee traditional buttercream (p. 146)
- ✓ patterned chocolate glaze (p. 151) made according to directions
- ✓ blue nonpareils and/or blue dragees (optional)
- ✓ ribbon 65 cm (26 in) and double-sided adhesive tape (optional)

Assembling and decorating the cake

1. Divide the cake layers and place the bottom cake layer on the board.
2. Brush each cake layer with coffee sugar syrup before you fill it and stack the next one.
3. Spread each cake layer with 125 ml (½ cup/4½ fl oz) of the milk chocolate ganache filling and then spread 125 ml (½ cup/4½ fl oz) of coffee buttercream over the ganache. (See filling and coating cakes p. 11.)
4. Coat the top and sides of the cake with the remaining 750 ml (3 cups/27 fl oz) of coffee buttercream and put it in the refrigerator for at least 15 minutes to set and chill.
5. Decorate the cake with patterned chocolate glaze and place the cake on a serving plate or cake stand. Put it in the refrigerator for 20-30 minutes for the glaze to set or leave at room temperature for a few hours or overnight.
6. If preferred, sprinkle blue nonpareils or dragees on the cake and place a few on the sides of the cake.
7. If preferred, fasten a ribbon around the bottom of the cake and attach the ends with double-sided adhesive tape after the glaze has set.
8. The cake can be kept at room temperature or refrigerated in an airtight container until 1 hour before serving.

Quick and easy version

Use only one type of filling instead of both milk chocolate ganache filling and coffee buttercream.

Cupcakes

1. Bake cupcakes using the recipe for almond butter cake (p. 115).
2. Cut a small hole into the top of each cupcake using an apple corer or a knife.
3. Brush each cupcake with coffee sugar syrup and spoon or pipe milk chocolate ganache or coffee buttercream into each cupcake.
4. Dip the top of each cupcake into dark chocolate glaze and make patterns with white and coloured chocolate on top.

Apple crumble cake

Apples in the cake batter and a crumble topping make a delicious dessert cake filled with layers of creamy custard and apple strudel.

Makes 12 slices

Toffee apples

- ✓ 1425 g (15 oz) can of baby apples
- ✓ 200 g (1 cup/7 oz) castor sugar

1. Drain the baby apples and dry them well with a kitchen towel.
2. Line a baking tray (sheet) with non-stick baking paper and spray with non-stick cooking spray.
3. Make a dry caramel with the sugar by heating the sugar in a pan on the stove at medium heat until the sugar turns an amber colour. I prefer to use a non-stick pan so that none of the sugar sticks to the edges of the pan.

4. Slowly stir the caramel with a wooden spoon while the sugar is melting to make sure that all the sugar crystals dissolve.
5. Immediately take the caramel off the heat when it turns an amber colour and all the sugar has dissolved. You can dip the bottom of the pan into a basin filled with ice water to stop the cooking process, if preferred, or pour the caramel into a microwave-safe glass bowl or silicon bakeware.

6. Be very careful when working with caramel as it is very hot and can burn your fingers! Keep a bowl of ice water nearby to dip your hand into in case you are splashed with hot caramel.
7. Working very quickly before the caramel starts to set, dip the dried baby apples into the caramel and place them on the lined tray.
8. If the caramel becomes too thick, you can heat it again at a low heat to liquefy it, or, if you have poured it into a microwave-safe glass bowl or silicon bakeware, heat it in a microwave oven for 20-30 seconds at a time until it has the consistency you prefer. Be careful not to overheat and burn the caramel.

9. Set your apples aside to use as decoration for the cake.

Tip

The toffee apples can be made a few hours in advance but do not keep them for too long as the toffee will start to melt. Do not refrigerate them.

Make the complete cake

- 2 round 20 cm (8 in) layers of apple crumble cake (p. 116)
- 1 round serving plate or cake stand
- ⅔ batch traditional custard filling (p. 139) or make a full batch and serve extra custard with the cake
- ½ batch fruit preserve filling: apple strudel variation (p. 134)
- a sprinkle of icing (confectioner's) sugar
- toffee apples made with 425 g (15 oz) can of baby apples and 200 g (1 cup/7 oz) castor sugar

Assembling and decorating the cake

1. Divide the cake layers and place one of the bottom layers on a serving plate or cake stand.
2. Spoon 250 ml (1 cup/9 fl oz) of the traditional custard filling onto the bottom cake layer making sure that the filling goes right up to the edges of the cake to show in the completed cake.
3. Place one of the top layers with the crumble topping on top of the custard.
4. Spoon all the apple strudel filling onto the crumble layer.
5. Repeat with the remaining bottom cake layer, spreading the rest or 250 ml (1 cup/9 fl oz) of the traditional custard filling on top. Use the remaining crumble layer as the last layer on top of the cake.
6. Sprinkle the top of the cake with a small amount of icing (confectioner's) sugar.
7. Arrange baby toffee apples on top of the cake.
8. The traditional custard filling is perishable; therefore keep the cake refrigerated in an airtight container until 1 hour before serving.
9. This cake can be served warm or cold. Heat the cake in an oven or in the microwave oven to serve warm.

Quick and easy version

- Decorate the cake with a sprinkling of icing (confectioner's) sugar only.
- Fill the cake with freshly whipped cream instead of custard.

Cupcakes

1. Bake cupcakes using the apple crumble cake recipe (p. 116).
2. Sprinkle the cupcakes with icing (confectioner's) sugar.
3. Decorate with a toffee apple.

Almond cake

The traditional frangipane or Bakewell tart is the inspiration for these layers of almond cake and almond paste filled with jam or fruit preserve. Macarons decorate the cake but you may use your chosen jam or fruit preserve as a topping instead.

Makes 12-16 slices

Macarons

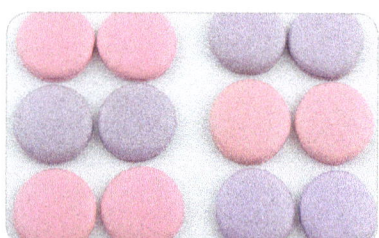

Your cake should be coated with a final coating of buttercream or ganache and placed on a serving plate or cake stand before proceeding with these steps.

- ✓ Macarons: I used 1½ batches or 75 macarons (p. 156). Colour ¾ batch pink and ¾ batch purple.
- ✓ Filling: 250 ml (1 cup/9 fl oz) meringue buttercream filling (p. 144) or traditional buttercream filling (p. 146) or white chocolate ganache filling (p. 130) mixed with 30 ml (2 T) strawberry, raspberry, cherry or pear fruit preserve (p. 133) or fruit jam
- ✓ Zip-lock bag or disposable piping bag

1. Make the 1½ batches of macarons according to the instructions on p. 156. Colour ¾ batch with pink or red food colouring and ¾ batch with purple (red and blue food colouring mixed together).
2. Dab some buttercream or ganache on the back of a single macaron and press it against the side of the cake right at the bottom. Proceed to attach 20 macarons around the bottom of the cake, alternating the colours.
3. Attach another row of 20 macarons on top of the first row, placing the alternating colours at an angle to form a slanting line.
4. Spoon the buttercream or ganache filling into a bag and snip off the tip to make a small hole.
5. Select 30 equal-sized macarons and on the back of half of them, pipe a blob of buttercream or ganache in the centre and not all the way to the edges.
6. Place another macaron on top of the filling and press and twist lightly to squeeze the filling towards the edges.
7. Make 15 filled macarons and place them on top of the cake using a drop of remaining buttercream or ganache to attach them, if necessary.

> ### Tip
> You could make the macarons a few days in advance. The filled or unfilled macarons will stay chewy for seven days in an airtight container in the refrigerator. If you leave them outside the refrigerator they will become dry and crunchy. They can also be frozen for 5-6 months. Bring back to room temperature before serving.

Make the complete cake

- ✓ 2 round 20 cm (8 in) layers of butter cake: almond variation (p. 115) or almond chocolate mud cake (p. 113)
- ✓ 1 round 20 cm (8 in) cake board or cardboard wrapped in foil or clingfilm
- ✓ 1 round serving plate or cake stand
- ✓ 60 ml (¼ cup/2¼ fl oz) almond-flavoured sugar syrup (p. 129)
- ✓ 1 batch strawberry, raspberry, cherry or pear fruit preserve (p. 133) or 375 ml (1½ cups/13½ fl oz) fruit jam
- ✓ 450 g (1 lb) purchased almond paste (marzipan)
- ✓ 1 batch white chocolate ganache coating (p. 149) or meringue buttercream (p. 144) or traditional buttercream (p. 146)
- ✓ macarons (p. 156), pre-made and filled with 250 ml (1 cup/9 fl oz) meringue buttercream (p. 144) or traditional buttercream (p. 146) or white chocolate ganache filling (p. 130) mixed with 30 ml (2 T) strawberry, raspberry, cherry or pear fruit preserve (p. 133) or fruit jam
- ✓ nonpareils (hundreds-and-thousands) (optional)

Assembling and decorating the cake

1. Roll out the almond paste (marzipan) on icing sugar until about 2-3 mm (⅛ in) thick.
2. Use your 20 cm (8 in) cake tin to cut out a circle from the almond paste with a sharp knife and the edge of the cake tin to guide you. Re-roll the off-cuts and cut out 2 more circles.
3. Divide the cake layers and place the bottom cake layer on the board.

4. Brush each cake layer with almond sugar syrup before you fill it and stack the next one.
5. Put a round of almond paste on each cake layer and spread 125 ml (½ cup/4½ fl oz) of fruit preserve or jam on top of the almond paste. Stack and fill each layer.
6. Coat the cake with the white chocolate ganache or buttercream. (See filling and coating cakes p. 11.)

7. Place the cake on a serving plate or cake stand and decorate it with macarons as described above. If preferred, sprinkle nonpareils on top of the cake.
8. The cake can be kept at room temperature or refrigerated in an airtight container until 1 hour before serving.

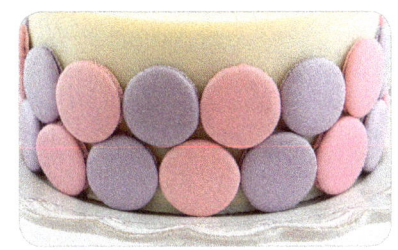

Quick and easy version

- Decorate the sides of the cake with flaked almonds as described on p. 90 and 93, rather than macarons.
- Decorate the top of the cake with fruit preserve or jam.

Cupcakes

1. Bake cupcakes using the almond butter cake (p. 115) or almond chocolate mud cake (p. 113) recipe.
2. Cut a small hole into the top of each cupcake using an apple corer or a knife.
3. Brush each cupcake with almond sugar syrup and spoon fruit preserve or jam filling and a piece of almond paste into each cupcake.
4. Spread the top of each cupcake with white chocolate ganache or buttercream coating.
5. Decorate with a macaron.

Chocolate mousse cake

Rich and creamy layers of dark chocolate mousse fill this dessert cake which is encased in an almond sponge collar. Grated chocolate and fresh berries complete the decoration.

Makes 12-16 slices

Chocolate almond sponge collar

The almond sponge is cut into strips to fit inside a 20 cm (8 in) cake tin to form a decorative collar around your cake.

- ✓ 1 batch decorative paste (see almond joconde recipe p. 126)
- ✓ 1 batch almond sponge cake: chocolate variation (p. 126)
- ✓ food colouring such as red and blue

1. Line your baking tray (sheet) with non-stick baking paper or a Silpat® mat. Make the decorative paste according to the recipe. Colour ⅓ of the paste with red food colouring and colour the rest light blue.
2. Spoon the red and light blue paste into small zip-lock bags or disposable piping bags. Snip off the tip off each bag.
3. Pipe light blue paste spirals all over the tray.
4. Pipe differently sized dots with red paste here and there on the tray.
5. Put the tray into a freezer for 20-30 minutes or until the paste is hard.
6. Mix the chocolate almond sponge batter according to the recipe instructions.
7. Take the tray out of the freezer and pour the batter over the design. Spread it thinly.
8. Bake the sponge for 7-8 minutes as per the recipe. When cool, invert it onto a piece of non-stick baking paper or clingfilm sprinkled with icing (confectioner's) sugar.
9. Measure the circumference of a round 20 cm (8 in) cake tin; it should be about 62 cm (25 in).
10. Cut the sponge in half lengthways. Cut each half into strips of 10 cm (4 in) wide and 32 cm (13 in) long.

11. Line the bottom and sides of the round baking tin with non-stick baking paper. The paper on the sides should be 10 cm (4 in) wide and stick out over the top edge of the tin. Spray with non-stick cooking spray.
12. Place the two sponge pieces inside the baking tin with the decorative pattern on the outside, against the paper lining. If the sponge strips stick to the baking paper or clingfilm they have been laid on, cut the paper or clingfilm to the size of each cake strip, pick them up as one and place into the tin before pulling off the backing paper or plastic.
13. Where the cake strips overlap, press them with your fingers to flatten them slightly. This will help to make the collar look like one continuous strip.
14. Cut any remaining pieces of sponge into blocks or with a cookie cutter to use as decorations on top of the cake.
15. Proceed to fill the cake.

Tip

You could make the collar a few days in advance. Wrap it in clingfilm and refrigerate until required.

Make the complete cake

- ✓ 2 round 20 cm (8 in) layers of chocolate fudge cake (p. 120) or dark chocolate mud cake (p. 112) or 6-8 layers of chocolate almond sponge cake (p. 126) cut into 20 cm (8 in) round discs
- ✓ 1 round 20 cm (8 in) cake board or cardboard wrapped in foil or clingfilm (optional)
- ✓ 1 round serving plate or cake stand
- ✓ 125 ml (½ cup/4½ fl oz) chocolate- or coffee-flavoured sugar syrup (p. 129); add brandy or Kahlua liqueur if preferred
- ✓ 1½ batches of dark chocolate mousse filling (p. 135), pre-made and set in the refrigerator
- ✓ chocolate almond sponge (p. 126) collar made according to directions
- ✓ fresh berries
- ✓ 50 g (1¾ oz) grated chocolate
- ✓ chocolate almond sponge cut-outs

Assembling and decorating the cake

1. Divide the cake layers or use 6-8 thin chocolate almond sponge layers. Ensure that they will fit inside the sponge collar in the cake tin by cutting off 5 mm (⅕ in) from the edge of each cake layer.

2. Place one cake layer in the bottom of the cake tin and brush with chocolate- or coffee-flavoured sugar syrup.
3. Spoon ⅓ or 310 ml (1¼ cup/11¼ fl oz) of the dark chocolate mousse on the cake layer and spread it evenly. Use less mousse if you have more layers, dividing it evenly.
4. Place the next cake layer on top and repeat until all the mousse and cake layers have been used. Place the last cake layer on top of the cake, making sure that it does not stick out above the sponge collar. Slice it off evenly with the collar if it does.
5. Put a serving plate, cake stand or a 20 cm (8 in) cake board on top of the cake and flip it over.
6. Carefully pull the cake tin off the cake and remove the non-stick baking paper. Brush the top cake layer with leftover chocolate or coffee sugar syrup.
7. Grate chocolate over the top of the cake and arrange fresh berries on the cake. Arrange decorative chocolate almond sponge cut-outs on top of the grated chocolate or berries.
8. The chocolate mousse filling is perishable; therefore keep the cake refrigerated in an airtight container until 1 hour before serving.

Note: If you prefer to use the chocolate mousse immediately after it has been made, pour the runny mousse onto the cake layers in the cake tin and refrigerate the cake for a few hours for the mousse to set before flipping it onto a serving plate or cake stand.

Quick and easy version

Leave out the almond sponge collar and stack the cake layers with chocolate mousse filling to let the filling show. Decorate with grated chocolate and fresh berries only.

Cupcakes

1. Bake cupcakes using the chocolate fudge cake (p. 120) or dark chocolate mud cake (p. 113) recipe.
2. Brush each cupcake with chocolate or coffee sugar syrup and spoon or pipe chocolate mousse filling onto each cupcake.
3. Decorate with cut-out decorative chocolate almond sponge pieces and fresh berries.

Milk tart cake

The warm and comforting flavour of a traditional South African milk tart is found in this dessert cake with its layers of condensed milk custard flavoured with cinnamon. Chocolate smears are used as decoration, as well as a light dusting of powdered cinnamon.

Makes 12-16 slices

Chocolate smears

✓ 100 g (3½ oz) of milk chocolate will make up to 22 smears.

1. Line a baking tray (sheet) with non-stick baking paper.
2. Melt the milk chocolate. Scoop a teaspoonful of the chocolate and drop it on the paper on the tray.
3. Stick an upside-down fork into the chocolate dollop and slide it towards you, lifting to make a smear with sharp points. Repeat until you have filled the paper with smears.
4. If it is a hot day put the tray with the chocolate in the refrigerator for no longer than 10 minutes, just to let the chocolate cool and set completely; otherwise let it set at room temperature.
5. Carefully peel the chocolate smears from the paper.

Tip

The chocolate smears can be made up to two weeks in advance. Store in an airtight container in a cool dark cupboard.

Make the complete cake

✓ 2 round 20 cm (8 in) layers of butter cake (p. 114)
✓ 1 round 20 cm (8 in) cake board or cardboard wrapped in foil or clingfilm
✓ 1 round serving plate or cake stand
✓ 1 batch condensed milk custard filling: milk tart variation (p. 138)
✓ ground cinnamon
✓ 1 batch white chocolate ganache coating: milk tart variation (p. 150) or milk tart traditional buttercream (p. 147)
✓ chocolate smears made with 100 g (3½ oz) milk chocolate
✓ small doilies or cake stencil
✓ cinnamon quills (optional)

Assembling and decorating the cake

1. Divide the cake layers and place the bottom cake layer on the board. Fill each layer before stacking the next on top.
2. Fill each cake layer with 250 ml (1 cup/9 fl oz) of the condensed milk custard filling.
3. Sprinkle each layer of filling with powdered cinnamon before placing the next layer of cake on top.
4. Coat the cake with milk tart-flavoured coating. (See filling and coating cakes p. 11.)
5. Place the cake on a serving plate or cake stand.
6. Make the chocolate smears as described above. Spread some coating on the back of each smear and press the smears against the side of the cake with the sharp points pointing upwards. Arrange smears all around the cake.
7. Cut out the centre part of each small doily and place the doilies or a cake stencil on top of the cake. Sprinkle powdered cinnamon over the doilies or cake stencil.
8. Remove the doilies or cake stencil to reveal the pattern.
9. If preferred, arrange cinnamon quills on top of the cake for decoration.
10. The condensed milk custard is perishable; therefore keep the cake refrigerated in an airtight container until 1 hour before serving.

Quick and easy version

- Use a purchased butter cake instead of baking one yourself.
- Omit the coating and spread the filling more thinly to have some left over to spread on top of the cake.
- If you do not have time to make chocolate smears, decorate this cake with cinnamon only.

Cupcakes

1. Bake butter cake cupcakes (p. 114).
2. Spoon milk tart-flavoured condensed milk custard filling into a zip-lock or disposable piping bag and pipe a swirl on each cupcake. Sprinkle with powdered cinnamon.
3. Decorate with a chocolate smear.

Tiramisu cake

A hint of coffee, creamy layers of mascarpone icing and a dusting of cocoa powder replicate the flavours found in a traditional tiramisu. Delicate chocolate curls are used as decoration.

Makes 12 slices

Chocolate curls

The chocolate curls for this project are made with 1 slab (90 g/3¼ oz) of white chocolate.

Tip
The chocolate curls can be made up to two weeks in advance and stored in an airtight container in a cool dark cupboard.

1. Break the slab of chocolate in half and place the pieces upside down on a dinner plate. Very lightly blow hot air over the chocolate with a hairdryer.
2. Heat the top for a few seconds only. Be careful not to blow too directly or too long on the chocolate, otherwise it will melt.
3. Hold the piece of chocolate upside down and pull a small, straight-edged knife over the top of the chocolate to form curls. Be very careful not to cut yourself by pulling the knife too fast.
4. If the chocolate is still too hard, the curls will crumble and if the chocolate is too warm, it will make one big shaving instead of a curl. If the chocolate is too cold, blow more hot air over it and if it is too hot and has melted slightly, just leave it to set and firm up again. Do not put it in the refrigerator.
5. Keep on peeling as many curls as you prefer.
6. Set the curls aside for decorating the cake.

Make the complete cake

- ✓ 2 round 17.5 cm (7 in) layers of butter cake: coffee variation (p. 115)
- ✓ 1 round 17.5 cm (7 in) cake board or cardboard wrapped in foil or cling wrap
- ✓ 1 round serving plate or cake stand
- ✓ 60 ml (¼ cup/2¼ fl oz) strong, cold coffee (do not use coffee-flavoured sugar syrup as it will make the cake too sweet)
- ✓ ¾ batch cream cheese icing: mascarpone variation (p. 148)
- ✓ cocoa powder
- ✓ ¾ batch dark chocolate ganache coating: coffee variation (p. 150) or coffee meringue buttercream (p. 145) or coffee traditional buttercream (p. 147)
- ✓ chocolate curls made with 1 slab (90 g/3¼ oz) of white chocolate
- ✓ chocolate balls such as Cadbury Whispers™
- ✓ gold dusting powder or edible crystals (optional)
- ✓ ribbon 58 cm (23 in) and double-sided adhesive tape (optional)

Assembling and decorating the cake

1. Divide the cake layers and place the bottom cake layer on the board.
2. Brush each layer with the strong, cold coffee before you fill it and stack the next one.
3. Spread 180 ml (¾ cup/6¾ fl oz) of the mascarpone icing on each cake layer and dust cocoa powder over the filling.
4. Coat the cake with the coffee-flavoured coating. Do not smooth the coating but spread it on quite roughly with your palette knife. (See filling and coating cakes p. 11.)
5. Place the cake on a serving plate or cake stand.
6. Make the chocolate curls as described above and spoon them onto the top of the cake.
7. For a special occasion, put gold dusting powder or edible crystals in your hand, roll the chocolate balls in the powder or glitter and arrange on top of the cake if you prefer.
8. If preferred, fasten a ribbon around the bottom of the cake and attach the ends with double-sided adhesive tape.
9. The mascarpone icing is perishable; therefore keep the cake refrigerated in an airtight container until 1 hour before serving.

Quick and easy version

Use plain mascarpone cheese mixed with a few teaspoons of icing (confectioner's) sugar instead of making mascarpone icing. Use crumbled Cadbury Flake™ chocolate instead of chocolate curls for decoration.

Cupcakes

1. Bake cupcakes using the coffee butter cake recipe (p. 115).
2. Brush each cupcake with strong, cold coffee and spoon or pipe mascarpone icing onto each cupcake.
3. Sprinkle cocoa powder over the mascarpone icing.
4. Decorate with white chocolate curls and chocolate balls.

Crème brûlée cake

Creamy custard and burnt sugar give the distinctive taste to this dessert cake which is enhanced with caramel shapes and caramel sprinkle. A blowtorch is used to burn the sugar.

Makes 12-16 slices

Caramel shapes and sprinkle

- 100 g (½ cup/3½ oz) castor sugar
- Nonpareils (hundreds-and-thousands)

1. Line a baking tray (sheet) with non-stick baking paper and spray with non-stick cooking spray.
2. Make a dry caramel with the sugar by heating the sugar in a pan on the stove at medium heat until the sugar turns an amber colour. I prefer to use a non-stick pan so that none of the sugar sticks to the edges of the pan.
3. Slowly stir the caramel with a wooden spoon while the sugar is melting to make sure that all the sugar crystals dissolve.
4. Immediately take the caramel off the heat when it turns an amber colour and all the sugar has melted.
5. Be very careful when working with caramel as it is very hot and can burn your fingers! Keep a bowl of ice water nearby to dip your hand into in case you are splashed with hot caramel.
6. Working quickly before the caramel starts to set, dip a teaspoon into the caramel and pour abstract shapes onto the paper-lined tray with the caramel.
7. For a whimsical twist, sprinkle each abstract shape with nonpareils before the caramel sets.
8. If the caramel becomes too thick, you can reheat it at a low heat on the stove to liquefy but be careful not to overheat and burn the caramel.
9. Use half the caramel shapes for decoration on the cake and process the rest in a food processor or place between two pieces of non-stick baking paper and smash with a rolling pin to make a coarsely ground sprinkle.
10. Set your caramel shapes and sprinkle aside to decorate the cake just before serving.

Tips

- The caramel shapes and sprinkle can be made a few days in advance and kept in an airtight container between layers of non-stick baking paper.
- Do not refrigerate the caramel shapes; place them on the cake just before serving as the caramel will become sticky and might melt slightly.

Make the complete cake

- ✓ 2 round 20 cm (8 in) layers of caramel butter cake (p. 115) or salted caramel cake (p. 122)
- ✓ 1 round 20 cm (8 in) cake board or cardboard wrapped in foil or clingfilm
- ✓ 1 round serving plate or cake stand
- ✓ 60 ml (¼ cup/2¼ fl oz) vanilla-flavoured sugar syrup (p. 128)
- ✓ 1 batch traditional custard filling (p. 139)
- ✓ 200 g (1 cup/7 oz) brown treacle or demerara sugar
- ✓ 1⅓ batch white chocolate ganache coating (p. 149) or 1⅓ batch traditional buttercream (p. 146)
- ✓ 1 batch white chocolate glaze (p. 151)
- ✓ caramel shapes and sprinkle made with 100 g (½ cup/3½ oz) castor sugar and nonpareils
- ✓ ribbon 65 cm (26 in) and double-sided adhesive tape (optional)

Assembling and decorating the cake

1. Divide the cake layers and place the bottom cake layer on the board.
2. Brush each layer with the vanilla sugar syrup before you fill it and stack the next one.
3. Pipe a circle around the edge of each cake layer with the white chocolate ganache coating or traditional buttercream, using 250 ml (1 cup/9 fl oz) in total for all three layers.
4. Fill each circle with 250 ml (1 cup/9 fl oz) of the traditional custard filling.
5. After each layer of filling, sprinkle the top of the custard with brown treacle sugar and caramelize it with a blowtorch. The burnt caramel will melt into the custard and cake layers to give the cake a deep caramel flavour. If you do not have a blowtorch, do not worry, the brown treacle sugar will melt into the custard.
6. Coat the top and sides of the cake with white chocolate ganache coating or traditional buttercream. Spread the coating slightly thinner than usual since the glaze will cover the coating. Put in the refrigerator for 15 minutes to chill and set.
7. If the prepared white chocolate glaze has set and is too firm to pour, reheat it in a microwave oven at 20% power or on the defrost setting until it is just above body temperature or runny enough to pour over the cake. It should

have the consistency of thin custard. Be careful not to overheat the glaze as it could melt the coating on the cake. It should be only slightly warmer than body temperature. Stir gently so that you do not incorporate too many air bubbles into the glaze.

8. Place the slightly chilled coated cake on a cooling rack over a baking tray (sheet) and pour the glaze over the cake preferably through a sieve, covering all the sides and moving the sieve and glaze towards the centre of the cake to cover the top.
9. If you see any air bubbles, quickly burst them with a sterilized pin or toothpick.
10. Scrape the glaze from the baking tray (sheet) and pour onto any sides of the cake that was not covered the first time or pour into a container to reuse for another project.

11. Carefully lift the cake from the cooling rack with an egg lifter, placing your other hand underneath the cake board and slide the cake onto a serving plate or cake stand with the egg lifter. Put the cake in the refrigerator for 20-30 minutes or leave at room temperature for a few hours for the glaze to set.
12. If preferred, fasten a ribbon around the bottom of the cake and attach the ends with double-sided adhesive tape after the glaze has set.
13. Sprinkle coarsely ground caramel and nonpareils in a wavy pattern on top of the cake and arrange caramel shapes on top for decoration. Prop the caramel shapes up with more crushed caramel if they lean backwards. Also stick a few caramel shapes on one side of the cake.

Quick and easy version

- Instead of using caramel shapes, sprinkle the coated cake with brown treacle sugar for decoration.
- Omit the vanilla sugar syrup and the white chocolate glaze if you prefer.

Cupcakes

1. Bake caramel butter (p. 115) or salted caramel (p. 122) cupcakes.
2. Cut a small hole into the top of each cupcake using an apple corer or a knife.
3. Brush each cupcake with vanilla sugar syrup and spoon or pipe traditional custard filling into and onto each cupcake.
4. Sprinkle brown treacle sugar over the custard filling and caramelize with a blowtorch.
5. Decorate with caramel shapes and caramel sprinkle.

Pineapple cheesecake

This tropical delight is filled with sweet and tangy layers of pineapple cream cheese icing and is decorated with colourful pineapple flowers and buttery biscuit crumble.

Makes 8-12 slices

Dried pineapple flowers

These pineapple flowers should be made at least one day in advance as they need to dry for quite a few hours. The dried pineapple flowers can be made up to four days in advance and kept in an airtight container in the refrigerator.

- ✓ 1 large fresh pineapple
- ✓ yellow and red liquid food colouring (optional)

1. Preheat your oven to 120 °C (250 °F) for a conventional oven or 100 °C (225 °F) for a fan-assisted oven.
2. Line a baking tray (sheet) with non-stick baking paper.
3. Peel the pineapple and remove all the 'eyes' and any brown spots.
4. Cut the pineapple into very thin slices; the thinner the slices the quicker they will dry. Dab the slices dry with kitchen towel if they are very juicy.
5. Cut away thin triangular slices from the outside flesh of the pineapple slices, leaving the inner core intact so that the pineapple slices will appear to have petals.
6. If preferred, mix 5 ml (1 t) yellow and 5 ml (1 t) red food colouring into 1 litre (4 cups/36 fl oz) water and soak some of the slices in the coloured water for about 1 hour to make dark orange-red pineapple slices. Dry the coloured slices with kitchen towel.
7. While the coloured slices are soaking thoroughly, place the plain slices on the baking tray and bake them for 20-30 minutes, depending on their thickness. Turn the slices over and bake them for another 20-30 minutes. If your slices are still not dry, turn them over again and check them at 10-minute intervals. Bake the optional coloured slices in the same way.
8. Remove them from the oven and place the warm slices into the hollows of a small to medium-sized muffin tin, depending on how wide your pineapple slices are. Keep in mind that they will shrink slightly while drying and the more they dry, the darker they will become.
9. Turn the oven off and put the muffin tin back in the oven. Leave the pineapple flowers in the oven until the oven is completely cool, or overnight.

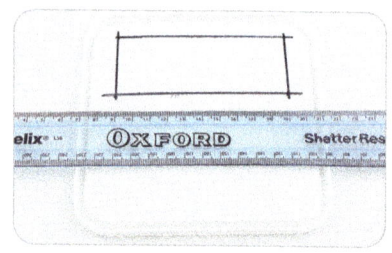

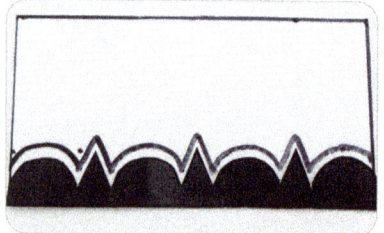

Decorative scraper

The decoration for the sides of the cake is made by cutting the lid of an ice cream or any other food-safe plastic container into a pattern and scraping the sides of the cake with it.

1. Draw a rectangle on the lid using a ruler and permanent marker as high as your stacked cake (about 10 cm (4 in) long and 5 cm (2 in) wide).
2. Cut out the rectangle with scissors.
3. Create your own pattern or use the pattern on the photo and enlarge it to 10 cm (4 in) long onto a piece of paper and cut it out. Place the cut-out pattern on the plastic rectangle and draw the outline onto it.
4. Cut out the plastic template with scissors.
5. Coat the cake with plain cream cheese icing (p. 148) with added lemon zest.
6. After scraping the icing into a smooth layer with the cake scraper or a long ruler, place the plastic template against the side of the cake and pull the patterned scraper in one smooth motion all around the cake to create a decorative pattern.
7. If you are not happy with the way it looks, spread leftover icing onto the cake, repeat scraping it into a smooth layer with the cake scraper and then repeat using the patterned plastic scraper to create a decorative pattern.

Make the complete cake

- ✓ 2 round 15 cm (6 in) layers of plain butter cake or pineapple variation (pp. 114-115)
- ✓ 1 round 15 cm (6 in) cake board or cardboard wrapped in foil or clingfilm
- ✓ 1 round serving plate or cake stand
- ✓ 1 batch cream cheese icing (p. 148), flavoured with lemon zest and divided between two bowls
- ✓ 60 g (¼ cup/2 oz) canned crushed or finely diced pineapple to add to half the cream cheese icing to use as filling
- ✓ 60 g (½ cup/2 oz) tea biscuits such as Tennis biscuits, Marie biscuits, ginger biscuits or shortbread
- ✓ 30 g (2 T/1 oz) salted butter or baking margarine, melted
- ✓ dried pineapple flowers (page 156)
- ✓ decorative scraper

Assembling and decorating the cake

1. Make a biscuit crumble by processing the tea biscuits in a food processor or with the processing attachment of a stick blender until it resembles fine crumbs, or put the biscuits into a plastic zip-lock bag and flatten them with a rolling pin. Stir the melted butter into the biscuit crumbs and set aside.
2. Divide the cake layers and place the bottom cake layer on a board. Fill each layer before stacking the next on top.
3. Fill each cake layer with 125 ml (½ cup/4½ fl oz) of the pineapple cream cheese icing and .
4. Spoon 2 tablespoons of biscuit crumbs onto each layer of filling.
5. Coat the cake with the plain cream cheese icing. (See filling and coating cakes p. 11.)
6. Create a decorative pattern on the sides of the cake with the patterned plastic scraper as described above and place the cake on a serving plate or cake stand.
7. Arrange dried pineapple flowers on top of the cake and sprinkle with biscuit crumble. Spoon the remaining biscuit crumble around the bottom edge of the cake.
8. Serve any extra pineapple flowers with each slice of cake.
9. The cream cheese icing is perishable; therefore keep the cake refrigerated in an airtight container until 1 hour before serving.

Quick and easy version

Decorate the cake with glacé pineapple pieces instead of making pineapple flowers.

Cupcakes

1. Bake cupcakes using the recipe for pineapple or plain butter cake (p. 114).
2. Spoon or pipe pineapple cream cheese icing onto each cupcake.
3. Decorate with biscuit crumbs and dried pineapple flowers.

Lime and coconut cake

The tartness of lime buttercream combines perfectly with toasted coconut and is enhanced by the sweetness of the coconut ice decorations.

Makes 12-16 slices

Easy striped coconut ice

I cut the coconut ice into 2 x 2 cm (¾ x ¾ in) blocks to make 100 squares. If you want to save time, cut it into bigger squares.

- 385 g can (1 cup/13¾ oz) sweetened condensed milk
- 400 g (3 cups/14 oz) icing (confectioner's) sugar
- 290 g (3½ cups/10 oz) unsweetened fine desiccated coconut
- a few drops of green and yellow food colouring

1. Line the bottom of a 20 cm (8 in) square or round tin or a small loaf tin with non-stick baking paper.
2. In a large bowl mix together the sweetened condensed milk, icing sugar and unsweetened fine desiccated coconut. If the mixture becomes too stiff to stir, knead it into a smooth ball.
3. Divide the mixture into two bowls and mix a few drops of green and yellow food colouring into one of the bowls, leaving the other plain. If the mixture feels too stiff, knead in the food colouring.
4. Divide each mixture again so that you have four separate balls of coconut ice.
5. Flatten each ball between two pieces of non-stick baking paper with a rolling pin. Roll it out until it is slightly bigger than the tin.
6. Place your tin on top of the rolled-out coconut ice and cut off any protruding pieces. Patch the cut-off pieces onto the corners of the rolled-out mixture if you are using a square or rectangular tin.
7. Cut all around the tin so that you are left with a flat piece of coconut ice the size of the tin.

8. Put a layer of white coconut ice into the tin and place a layer of the coloured coconut ice on top. Press it with your fingers to make it stick to the white layer. Repeat with the other two pieces of coconut ice to make four layers.

9. If the coconut ice layers dried out while you were rolling out each colour, rub a few drops of water on each layer before placing the next into the tin to make sure that they stick together. Do not add too much water as this can soften the coconut ice and make it too sticky.

10. Refrigerate the coconut ice for 2 hours or until set.

11. Tip the coconut ice out onto a cutting board and cut it into small blocks with a small serrated paring knife, using a sawing motion. The sawing motion will prevent the colours from blending into each other. Press any loose pieces of coconut ice back into each block with your fingers.

> *Tip*
>
> The coconut ice will keep for two weeks in an airtight container.

Make the complete cake

- ✓ 2 round 20 cm (8 in) layers of butter cake: coconut variation (p. 115) or coconut chocolate mud cake (p. 113)
- ✓ 1 round 20 cm (8 in) cake board or cardboard wrapped in foil or clingfilm or a round serving plate or cake stand
- ✓ 125 ml (½ cup/4½ fl oz) lime-flavoured sugar syrup (p. 129); if preferred, add coconut liqueur to the sugar syrup and use lemons if no limes are available
- ✓ 2 batches of lime meringue buttercream (p. 145); use lemons if you cannot find limes
- ✓ 30 g (6 T/1 oz) unsweetened desiccated coconut
- ✓ easy striped coconut ice made according to directions
- ✓ 80 g (1 cup/2¾ oz) coconut shavings made from coconut chunks or a fresh coconut; if you cannot find fresh coconut, decorate the cake with unsweetened desiccated coconut instead

Assembling and decorating the cake

1. Put the unsweetened desiccated coconut in a microwave-safe bowl and heat it in a microwave oven at 50% power, stirring at 30-second intervals until the coconut is toasted and golden brown.

2. Make coconut shavings from coconut chunks or a fresh coconut broken into chunks. Use a vegetable peeler and leave a small rind of brown skin attached to the flesh.

3. Divide the cake layers and place the bottom cake layer on a board, serving plate or cake stand.
4. Brush each layer liberally with lime sugar syrup before you fill it and stack the next one.
5. Fill each cake layer with 250 ml (1 cup/9 fl oz) of the lime buttercream and spoon 2 tablespoons of toasted coconut over the filling.
6. Coat the cake with the remaining lime buttercream. Use your palette knife to spread the coating into a rough uneven layer instead of making it perfectly smooth. (See filling and coating cakes p. 11.)
7. Spoon the coconut shavings into your hand and press them halfway up the sides of the cake.
8. Arrange the blocks of coconut ice on top of the cake and add a few coconut shavings.
9. If you used lime curd to make the lime buttercream, keep the cake refrigerated in an airtight container until 1 hour before serving.

Quick and easy version

- Use store-bought coconut marshmallows as decoration instead of making the striped coconut ice.
- Decorate the cake with unsweetened desiccated coconut instead of coconut shavings.

Cupcakes

1. Bake cupcakes using the coconut butter cake (p. 115) or coconut chocolate mud cake (p. 113) recipe.
2. Brush each cupcake with lime sugar syrup and spoon or pipe lime buttercream onto each cupcake.
3. Decorate with coconut shavings and coconut ice.

Lemon and raspberry cake

Layers of tangy lemon curd and soft, creamy raspberry buttercream fill this dessert cake. If you cannot find raspberries, use strawberries instead. You could also substitute the lemons with oranges.

Makes 16-20 slices

Rice Krispie bars

The Rice Krispie bars are cut into thin strips of 7.5 cm (3 in) high and 3 cm (1¼ in) wide to attach around the cake. This recipe makes 38 bars; you will need 24 bars to arrange around the cake.

- ✓ 150 g (3 cups/5¼ oz) marshmallows
- ✓ 30 g (2 T/1 oz) salted butter or baking margarine
- ✓ 150 g (3 cups/5¼ oz) Rice Krispies
- ✓ nonpareils (hundreds-and-thousands)

1. Line a baking tray (sheet) with non-stick baking paper and spray with cooking spray.
2. Assemble your ingredients.
3. Put the marshmallows and butter in a microwave-safe bowl and microwave on high for 2 minutes, stirring at 30-second intervals or until melted and smooth.
4. Stir the Rice Krispies into the melted marshmallow mixture.
5. Press the Rice Krispie mixture into the baking tray using buttered hands to press it down into a thin layer.
6. Sprinkle nonpareils over the surface of the Rice Krispie mixture in the tray.
7. Leave to cool for about 30 minutes and then lift it out of the baking tray with an egg lifter and onto a cutting board.
8. Dip a sharp knife into just-boiled water and dry thoroughly to cut through the sticky Rice Krispies. Keep on dipping the knife and drying it as necessary.

9. Measure the Rice Krispie layer from the top into three 7.5 cm (3 in) sections and cut it in thirds lengthwise. Place a ruler of about 3 cm (1¼ in) wide on top of each section and cut small bars using the width of the ruler as a guide or measure each long strip into smaller 3 cm (1¼ in) sections and cut into small bars with a knife.
10. Leave the Rice Krispie bars overnight to firm and arrange around the cake for decoration.

Tip

The Rice Krispie bars can be made up to one week in advance and stored in an airtight container in a cool dark cupboard.

Make the complete cake

- ✓ 2 round 22 cm (9 in) layers of raspberry butter cake (p. 115) or raspberry chocolate mud cake (p. 113)
- ✓ 1 round 22 cm (9 in) cake board or cardboard wrapped in foil or clingfilm
- ✓ 1 round serving plate or cake stand
- ✓ 80 ml (⅓ cup/3 fl oz) lemon-flavoured sugar syrup (p. 129) or limoncello liqueur
- ✓ 1 batch of lemon curd (p. 132)
- ✓ 1½ batches of raspberry meringue buttercream (p. 145) or raspberry traditional buttercream (p. 147)
- ✓ Rice Krispie bars made according to directions
- ✓ 250 g (2 cups/9 oz) fresh raspberries
- ✓ ribbon 72 cm (29 in) and double-sided adhesive tape (optional)

Assembling and decorating the cake

1. Divide the cake layers and place the bottom cake layer on the board.
2. Brush each layer with the lemon sugar syrup before you fill it and stack the next one.

3. Thinly spread the first three cake layers with 125 ml (½ cup/4½ fl oz) of raspberry buttercream.
4. Pipe a thick circle around the edge of each cake layer, using 250 ml (1 cup/9 fl oz) of the raspberry buttercream in total for all three layers.
5. Fill each of these circles with 250 ml (1 cup/9 fl oz) of the lemon curd filling.
6. Coat the cake with the remaining raspberry buttercream. (See filling and coating cakes p. 11.)
7. Place the cake on a serving plate or cake stand.
8. Make the Rice Krispie bars as described above and press them against the buttercream on the sides of the cake.
9. If preferred, fasten a ribbon around the cake and tie it into a bow.
10. Arrange fresh raspberries on top of the cake.
11. The lemon curd and fresh raspberries are perishable items; therefore keep the cake refrigerated in an airtight container until 1 hour before serving.

Quick and easy version

Omit the Rice Krispie bars.

Cupcakes

1. Bake cupcakes using the raspberry butter cake (p. 115) or raspberry chocolate mud cake (p. 113) recipe.
2. Cut a small hole into the top of each cupcake using an apple corer or a knife.
3. Brush each cupcake with lemon sugar syrup and spoon or pipe lemon curd filling into each cupcake using a zip-lock or disposable piping bag.
4. Spread the top of each cupcake with raspberry buttercream or pipe a dollop of buttercream on each cupcake.
5. Decorate with fresh raspberries and a small Rice Krispie bar.

Passionfruit cake

Delectable sweet and sour passionfruit curd is used as a filling for this dessert cake.

Makes 12 slices

Lace decoration

- 60 cm (24 in) lace fabric, washed and dried
- 60 cm (24 in) ribbon
- double-sided adhesive tape

Prepare and coat the cake beforehand.

1. To cut your piece of lace fabric, measure the height and circumference of the cake. Subtract ¼ from the height and add 4 cm (1²⁄₃ in) to the circumference for an overlap. The lace should be about 7.5 cm (3 in) wide and 60 cm (24 in) long.
2. Cut a piece of double-sided adhesive tape for one edge of the lace fabric and stick it to the fabric. Remove the protective plastic from the tape.
3. Fold the lace around the cake and place the end with the double-sided tape on top of the other lace end.
4. Repeat this with the ribbon, bringing the ends of the ribbon together where the ends of the lace meet.

Make the complete cake

- 2 round 17.5 cm (7 in) layers of butter cake: passionfruit variation (p. 115)
- 1 round 17.5 cm (7 in) cake board or cardboard wrapped in foil or cling wrap
- 1 round serving plate or cake stand
- 60 ml (¼ cup/2¼ fl oz) passionfruit-flavoured sugar syrup (p. 129)
- ¾ batch passionfruit curd filling (p. 132)
- 1 batch meringue buttercream (p. 144) or traditional buttercream coating (p. 146) coloured yellow
- lace decoration made with:
    60 cm (24 in) lace fabric, washed and dried
    60 cm (24 in) ribbon and double-sided adhesive tape
- mini meringues made from ½ a batch of meringue mixture (p. 153)

- ✓ 30 ml (2 T) passionfruit pulp
- ✓ gooseberries (optional)

Assembling and decorating the cake

1. Divide the cake layers and place the bottom cake layer on a board.
2. Brush each layer with the passionfruit sugar syrup before you fill it and stack the next one.
3. Pipe a thick circle around the edge of each cake layer with the yellow buttercream, using 180 ml (¾ cup/6¾ fl oz) in total for all three layers.
4. Fill each cake layer with 180 ml (¾ cup/6¾ fl oz) of the passionfruit curd filling.

5. Coat the cake with the remaining 560 ml (2¼ cups/20¼ fl oz) of yellow buttercream. (See filling and coating cakes p. 11.)
6. Decorate the cake with lace fabric and ribbon as described above.
7. Place the cake on a serving plate or cake stand.
8. Spoon 30 ml (2 T) passionfruit pulp around the top edge of the cake and arrange the mini meringues on top of the cake just before serving. If preferred, decorate the cake with fresh gooseberries to complement the yellow colour of the passionfruit.
9. The passionfruit curd is a perishable item; therefore keep the cake refrigerated in an airtight container until 1 hour before serving.

Quick and easy version

Omit the lace and ribbon decoration; pour extra passionfruit pulp around the bottom of the cake on the serving plate or cake stand.

Cupcakes

1. Bake cupcakes using the recipe for passionfruit butter cake (p. 115).
2. Cut a small hole into the top of each cupcake using an apple corer or a knife.
3. Brush each cupcake with passionfruit sugar syrup and spoon or pipe passionfruit curd into each cupcake using a zip-lock or disposable piping bag.
4. Pipe a swirl of plain yellow buttercream on top of each cupcake.
5. Decorate with passionfruit pulp and mini meringues.

Apricot and coconut meringue cake

This dessert cake was inspired by traditional South African Hertzog tarts. The cake is baked with coconut meringue on top and filled with a thick layer of apricot preserve.

Makes 12 slices

Mini macarons

Makes 45 sandwiched French macarons.

- ½ a batch of macaron mixture (p. 156)
- Orange food colouring (mix together yellow and red food colouring if you do not have orange)
- 60 ml (¼ cup/2¼ fl oz) traditional buttercream mixed with 5 ml (1 t) chunky apricot jam or 1.25 ml (¼ t) filling per sandwiched macaron

1. Make ½ batch of macaron mixture as described on p. 156.
2. Divide the mixture into two bowls and colour one bowl light orange and one bowl dark orange. You could also mix some of each mixture together to make marbled macarons.
3. Pipe small 2 cm (¾ in) rounds of macaron mixture and bake according to the instructions.
4. Sandwich the mini macarons together with 1.25 ml (¼ t) buttercream per sandwiched macaron.

Make the complete cake

- 2 round 20 cm (8 in) layers coconut meringue cake (p. 118)
- 1 round serving plate or cake stand
- 1 batch fruit preserve: chunky apricot jam variation (p. 133) or 375 ml (1½ cup/13½ fl oz) chunky apricot jam
- 135 g (9 T/4¾ oz) dried Turkish apricots, chopped into small pieces
- 80 ml (⅓ cup/3 fl oz) traditional buttercream (p. 146)
- 45 mini macarons made using ½ a batch of macaron mixture (p. 156) and filled with 60 ml (¼ cup/4¼ fl oz) traditional buttercream mixed with 5 ml (1 t) chunky apricot jam
- 30 ml (2 T) traditional buttercream to paste mini macarons to the top of the cake

Assembling and decorating the cake

1. Gently lift the cold cake layers from the cake tins without tipping them out, otherwise the coconut meringue will flatten and crumble. Carefully divide each cake layer in two.
2. Place a bottom cake layer on a serving plate or cake stand and spread it with 125 ml (½ cup/4½ fl oz) chunky apricot jam fruit preserve or chunky apricot jam.
3. Spoon 2 tablespoons of chopped Turkish apricots over the filling and place one of the cake's top layers on the jam filling.
4. Pipe an icing circle with the traditional buttercream coating all around the edge of the layer over the coconut meringue and fill the circle with 125 ml (½ cup/4½ fl oz) chunky apricot jam fruit preserve or chunky apricot jam. Spoon 2 tablespoons of chopped Turkish apricots over the filling.
5. Press another 2 tablespoons of chopped Turkish apricots into the buttercream circle.
6. Place the second bottom cake layer on top and spread it with the last 125 ml (½ cup/4½ fl oz) of chunky apricot jam fruit preserve or chunky apricot jam. Spoon 2 tablespoons of Turkish apricots over the filling and place the last coconut meringue layer on top.
7. Spoon 30 ml (2 T) traditional buttercream into a small zip-lock bag and snip off a corner to make a piping bag. Pipe a small dollop on a few of the mini macarons and press them onto the top of the cake.
8. Decorate the top of the cake with the last tablespoon of chopped apricots and arrange the remaining mini macarons all around the cake. Serve each slice of cake with 4 mini macarons.

Quick and easy version

- Omit the buttercream icing circle and Turkish apricot decoration.
- Omit the mini macarons and decorate the cake with whole Turkish apricots or apricot sweets instead.

Cupcakes

1. Bake cupcakes using the coconut meringue cake recipe (p. 118).
2. Spoon chunky apricot preserve or chunky apricot jam onto each cupcake.
3. Arrange chopped Turkish apricots and mini macarons on top.

Hazelnut cake

Celebrated Ferrero Rocher™ chocolates are the inspiration for this dessert cake, filled with decadent layers of hazelnut ganache.

Makes 16-20 slices

Stencilling

When the cake is coated with buttercream or ganache and ready to be decorated, follow the remainder of the steps.

- ✓ 60-125 ml (¼-½ cup/2¼-4½ fl oz) traditional buttercream coloured pink. The amount required will depend on the size of the pattern on the stencil.
- ✓ purchased stencil, e.g. from www.elementals.co.za or www.yuppiechef.com (www.lindyscakes.co.uk (UK)/www.designer-stencils.com (USA))

1. Put the cake in the freezer for 15 minutes or in the refrigerator for 30 minutes for the coating to chill and set. If you have used a buttercream coating, make sure that it feels very firm to the touch.
2. If your pink buttercream feels too stiff, soften it slightly with a few drops of water to a spreadable, peanut butter-like consistency.
3. Carefully place the stencil against the cake and lightly hold it in place on the side of the cake.
4. Using a palette knife or offset spatula, put a dollop of buttercream on the stencil and spread it over the stencil. Depending on the size of your stencil, add more buttercream if necessary to cover the stencil pattern. When you put the buttercream on the stencil it will hold the stencil in place.
5. Scrape off the excess buttercream to leave a thin layer.
6. Remove the stencil from the cake to reveal the pattern.
7. Decorate the entire circumference of the cake by repeating the stencil design.

Tip
Make your own stencil by tracing a pattern onto non-stick baking paper. There are many pattern ideas on the internet.

Make the complete cake

- ✓ 2 round 22 cm (9 in) layers chocolate fudge cake (p. 120) or chocolate mud cake: dark chocolate variation (p. 113)
- ✓ 1 round 22 cm (9 in) cake board or cardboard wrapped in foil or clingfilm
- ✓ 1 round serving plate or cake stand
- ✓ 1¼ batch milk chocolate ganache filling: hazelnut variation (p. 131), with 30 ml (2 T) hazelnut liqueur such as Frangelico added (optionally)
- ✓ 1¼ batch milk chocolate ganache coating (p. 149) or 1¼ batch of hazelnut traditional buttercream (p. 147)
- ✓ Stencilling as described above

- ✓ Ferrero Rocher™ chocolates or chocolate-coated nuts
- ✓ rose petals (optional)
- ✓ ribbon 73 cm (29 in) and double-sided adhesive tape (optional)

Assembling and decorating the cake

1. Divide the cake layers and place the bottom cake layer on a board.
2. Fill each of the cake layers with 310 ml (1¼ cups/11¼ fl oz) of the hazelnut milk chocolate ganache filling before you stack the next one.
3. Coat the cake with milk chocolate ganache coating or hazelnut traditional buttercream. (See filling and coating cakes p. 11.)
4. Decorate the sides of the cake by applying pink buttercream over the stencil to create a pattern on the cake.
5. Place the cake on a serving plate or cake stand.
6. For a special occasion you may want to place pink rose petals on top of the cake.
7. Arrange the Ferrero Rocher™ chocolates or chocolate-coated nuts on the top of the cake.
8. If preferred, secure a ribbon around the bottom of the cake and attach the ends with double-sided adhesive tape.

Quick and easy version

- Do not use coating but let the filling show. Spread the hazelnut ganache filling slightly thinner and spread the remaining filling on top of the cake.
- Omit the stencil decoration.

Cupcakes

1. Bake chocolate fudge (p. 120) or dark chocolate mud (p. 113) cupcakes.
2. Cut a small hole into the top of each cupcake using an apple corer or a knife.
3. Spoon or pipe hazelnut milk chocolate ganache filling into each cupcake using a zip-lock or disposable piping bag.
4. Spread the top of each cupcake with milk chocolate ganache coating or hazelnut-flavoured traditional buttercream coating.
5. Decorate with a stencil pattern and a Ferrero Rocher™ chocolate.

Black forest-inspired cake

Cherries are the theme for this black forest-inspired dessert cake filled with creamy layers of cherry buttercream and cherry preserve.

Makes 12 slices

Sprinkled marshmallows

The recipe makes 40 marshmallows of about 4 cm (1²/₃ in) wide. You will only need 15 marshmallows to decorate the sides of the cake. Serve the rest of the marshmallows with each slice of cake. The marshmallows could be sprinkled with nonpareils (hundreds-and-thousands) or chopped nuts or, to keep them plain, sift a mixture of icing (confectioner's) sugar and cornflour (cornstarch) over the surface of the marshmallows.

For the sprinkle
- ✓ 30 g (¹/₃ cup/1 oz) unsweetened desiccated coconut
- ✓ 20 g (2 T/¾ oz) dried cherries, dried cranberries or crimson raisins

For the marshmallows
- ✓ 15 ml (1 T) gelatine powder
- ✓ 60 ml (¼ cup/2¼ fl oz) water
- ✓ 130 g (1 cup/4²/₃ oz) icing (confectioner's) sugar
- ✓ 15 ml (1 T) golden syrup, honey or liquid glucose (light corn syrup)
- ✓ 60 ml (¼ cup/2¼ fl oz) water
- ✓ 5 ml (1 t) vanilla essence
- ✓ 1 large egg white
- ✓ 15 ml (1 T) icing (confectioner's) sugar mixed with 15 ml (1 T) cornflour (cornstarch)

1. Put the unsweetened desiccated coconut and the dried cherries, cranberries or crimson raisins in a food processor and pulse until it looks like breadcrumbs. If you do not have a food processor, chop into tiny pieces on a chopping board. Set aside to use later.
2. Prepare 2-3 pieces of non-stick baking paper by marking lines with a ruler and permanent marker to create 5 cm (2 in) strips. Leave a 1 cm (½ in) space between each strip so that the marshmallows do not touch each other.
3. Turn the paper over so that the marks are underneath and line 2-3 baking trays (sheets) with the paper. Brush a thin layer of vegetable oil over the paper.
4. Assemble your ingredients. Sprinkle the gelatine powder over 60 ml (¼ cup/2¼ fl oz) of water and leave to bloom.
5. In a small saucepan or pot, mix together the icing sugar, syrup, honey or glucose and 60 ml (¼ cup/2¼ fl oz) of water. Heat the mixture on a stove on medium heat, stirring until it comes to a rolling boil. Boil for 2 minutes only.
6. Remove the saucepan from the heat, stir in the bloomed gelatine to dissolve it and add the vanilla essence.

7. In a large bowl, whisk the egg white with a handheld electric beater or standing mixer on medium speed to soft peak stage and then slowly pour the hot liquid in a stream into the bowl while whisking continuously.
8. Whisk for another 5-7 minutes until the mixture has cooled slightly and has thickened. It should still be soft enough to pipe or spread out. As the mixture cools it will start to set.
9. Spoon half the mixture into a large zip-lock or a disposable piping bag and cut a small hole of about 1 cm (½ in) into one tip.
10. Pipe two sets of lines of about 4 cm (1²⁄₃ in) wide like a big M up and down against each other, staying inside the lines drawn on the paper.
11. When one tray is full, quickly pour some of the sprinkle-mixture over the marshmallows while the surface is still sticky.
12. If the rest of the marshmallow mixture in the bowl has started to set, microwave it on high for 10-20 seconds to soften and spoon it into the bag. Pipe more lines up and down until all of the mixture has been used and sprinkle with the remaining sprinkle mixture.
13. If you do not want to pipe the marshmallow mixture, you could pour it onto a lined tray and smooth it with a non-stick spatula. Sprinkle with the sprinkle mixture and when it has set, cut it into blocks with an oiled knife. Arrange the blocks around the sides of the cake.
14. Set the marshmallows aside for 6 hours or overnight to set and dry out slightly. Dip your fingers into the icing sugar and cornflour mixture when lifting the marshmallows off the paper.
15. Use the marshmallows to decorate the sides of the cake.

Tip

The sprinkled marshmallows can be made up to a week in advance. To store them, sift a mixture of icing (confectioner's) sugar and cornflour (cornstarch) over non-stick baking paper in an airtight container and put the marshmallows on the icing sugar mixture.

Make the complete cake

- ✓ 2 round 17.5 cm (7 in) layers of plain butter cake (p. 114) or plain chocolate mud cake (p. 112)
- ✓ 1 round 17.5 cm (7 in) cake board or cardboard wrapped in foil or cling wrap
- ✓ 1 round serving plate or cake stand
- ✓ 60 ml (¼ cup/2¼ fl oz) liqueur-flavoured sugar syrup (p. 129) made with cherry or Kirsch liqueur or use the drained juice from a can of cherries for an alcohol-free, less-sweet syrup
- ✓ ½ batch cherry fruit preserve (p. 133) (I used canned black cherries in my fruit preserve)
- ✓ 1½ batches cherry meringue buttercream (p. 145) or cherry traditional buttercream (p. 147)
- ✓ sprinkled marshmallows made according to directions above
- ✓ fresh, canned, glacé or maraschino cherries

Assembling and decorating the cake

1. Divide the cake layers and place the bottom cake layer on a board.
2. Brush each layer with the liqueur sugar syrup before you fill it and stack the next one.
3. Thinly spread each of the first three cake layers with 125 ml (½ cup/4½ fl oz) of cherry buttercream.
4. Pipe a thin circle around the edge of each cake layer, using 125 ml (½ cup/4½ fl oz) of the cherry buttercream in total for all three layers.
5. Fill each of the circles with 125 ml (½ cup/4½ fl oz) of the cherry fruit preserve filling.
6. Coat the cake with the remaining 625 ml (2½ cups/22½ fl oz) of cherry buttercream. (See filling and coating cakes p. 11.)
7. Place the cake on a serving plate or cake stand.
8. Make the sprinkled marshmallows as described above and press them against the sides of the cake.
9. Arrange fresh, canned, glacé or maraschino cherries on top of the cake.
10. The cherry fruit preserve is a perishable item; therefore keep the cake refrigerated in an airtight container until 1 hour before serving.

Quick and easy version

- Omit the cherry fruit preserve filling if you prefer and use cherry buttercream as a filling and coating.
- Omit the sprinkled marshmallows.

Cupcakes

1. Bake cupcakes using the plain butter cake (p. 114) or plain chocolate mud cake (p. 112) recipe.
2. Cut a small hole into the top of each cupcake using an apple corer or a knife.
3. Spoon cherry fruit preserve filling into each cupcake.
4. Spread the top of each cupcake with cherry buttercream.
5. Decorate with a sprinkled marshmallow and a cherry.

Trifle cake

This dessert cake, filled with layers of custard, jelly and chopped nuts, is inspired by traditional Christmas trifle. Whether you make this for Christmas or for any day of the week, it is sure to bring back fond memories. Add canned fruit, glacé fruit or maraschino cherries if you prefer.

Makes 12-16 slices

Candied pecan nuts

The pecan nut sprinkle used in the decorative cake border is made from candied pecan nuts. These sweet and salty pecan nuts are the ultimate snack food. The pecan nuts can be substituted with any other nuts you prefer.

Makes 200 g (2 cups/7 oz) of candied pecan nuts.

- ✓ 1 large egg white
- ✓ 5 ml (1 t) vanilla essence
- ✓ 200 g (2 cups/7 oz) pecan nut halves
- ✓ 100 g (½ cup/3½ oz) brown treacle or demerara sugar
- ✓ 2.5 ml (½ t) fine table salt
- ✓ An extra pinch or two of fine table salt

1. Assemble your ingredients and pre-heat your oven to 140 °C (285 °F).
2. Line a baking tray (sheet) with non-stick baking paper.
3. Whisk the egg white and vanilla essence lightly and then add the pecan nuts. Make sure that all the nuts are coated with the egg white.
4. Put the brown treacle sugar and salt into a clean bowl. Spoon the coated pecan nuts into the sugar mixture.
5. Pour the sugar-coated nuts onto the prepared baking tray and spread them out into an even layer. Sprinkle the nuts with an extra pinch or two of salt.
6. Bake the nuts for 45 minutes, stirring them every 15 minutes.
7. Remove the nuts from the oven and let them cool on the tray.

Tip

The candied pecan nuts can be made up to two weeks in advance and stored in an airtight container.

Decorative cake border

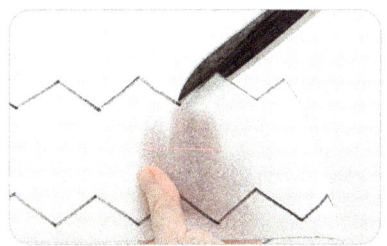

- ✓ To make the sprinkle for the decorative cake border, crush a portion of 50 g (½ cup/1¾ oz) of the candied nuts into small pieces with a food processor or, if you do not have a food processor, put the candied nuts in a bag and smash them with a hammer or a meat mallet. Keep the rest of the candied pecan nuts whole to decorate the cake and to serve with the cake.
- ✓ Of course, instead of the chopped candied nuts, you could also use any edible items such as flaked almonds, chocolate vermicelli (sprinkles), nonpareils (hundreds-and-thousands), praline, peanut brittle, chocolate shavings, cake crumbs or cookie crumbs.
- ✓ Cut out any pattern from non-stick baking paper to use as a decorative pattern around the cake.

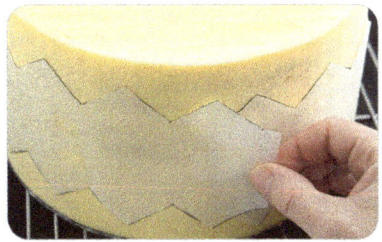

Your cake should be coated with a final layer of coating and chilled before starting with this technique.

1. Make a template for the decorative pattern by determining the exact size of the collar you need to cover the cake:
   - Measure the height of the cake;
   - Measure the circumference of the cake;
   - Cut a piece of non-stick baking paper to this size.

2. Draw any pattern such as a zigzag about 2.5 cm (1 in) wide from the top and the bottom edge of the paper and cut it out with scissors. Spray non-stick cooking spray on the side of the paper template which will be against the cake.
3. Place your coated cake on a cooling rack with a baking tray (sheet) underneath to catch any sprinkle that might fall off.

4. Fold the paper template around the cake, positioning it around the middle. Stick the ends together with adhesive tape.
5. Spread a thin layer of leftover coating on the open areas for the sprinkle to adhere to.
6. Spoon some of the pecan nut sprinkle into your hand and press it against the open areas at the edges of the cake. Repeat until all the open areas have been covered.

7. Loosen the adhesive tape and remove the paper from the cake to reveal the patterns. If the paper sticks to the coating, put the cake in a refrigerator for 30 minutes or in a freezer for 15 minutes for the coating to set before removing the paper.

Make the complete cake

- 2 round 20 cm (8 in) layers plain butter cake (p. 114) or plain chocolate mud cake (p. 112)
- 1 round 20 cm (8 in) cake board or cardboard wrapped in foil or clingfilm
- 1 round serving plate or cake stand
- 60 ml (¼ cup/2¼ fl oz) sherry or brandy-flavoured sugar syrup (p. 129)
- ½ batch traditional custard (p. 139)
- ½ packet of red and ½ packet of green jelly made according to the packet instructions
- 5 whole green glacé cherries and 5 whole red glacé cherries, chopped or 15 ml (1 T) each
- 50 g (½ cup/1¾ oz) chopped candied pecan nuts
- 1⅓ batch white chocolate ganache coating (p. 149) or 1⅓ batch meringue (p. 144) or traditional (p. 146) buttercream
- decorative cake border made with:
    non-stick baking paper
    50 g (½ cup/1¾ oz) candied pecan nut sprinkle
- 25 g (2 T/1 oz) whole candied pecan nuts
- a few red and green glacé cherries
- glacé fruits (optional)
- gold dragées (optional)

Assembling and decorating the cake

1. Slice the set jellies into cubes and set aside 1 tablespoon of each colour to use later.
2. Divide the cake layers and place the bottom cake layer on the board.
3. Brush each layer with the sherry- or brandy-flavoured sugar syrup before you fill it and stack the next one.
4. Pipe a circle around the edge of each cake layer with the white chocolate ganache coating or buttercream to create a barrier for the custard and jelly, using 250 ml (1 cup/9 oz) in total for all three layers.
5. Fill each cake layer with 125 ml (½ cup/4½ fl oz) of the traditional custard filling. Spoon green jelly and green glacé cherries onto the custard on the bottom cake layer.

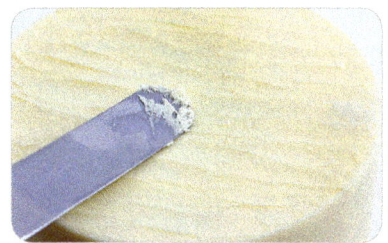

6. Spoon chopped candied pecan nuts onto the middle custard layer and spoon red jelly cubes and red glacé cherries on the last custard layer.
7. Coat the cake with the remaining 750 ml (3 cups/27 fl oz) of white chocolate ganache coating or buttercream. Spread the coating on the top of the cake from side to side with a palette knife to create texture. (See filling and coating cakes p. 11.)
8. Make the decorative border as described above.
9. Place the cake on a serving plate or cake stand.
10. Arrange whole candied pecan nuts, glacé cherries and optional glacé fruits on top of the cake in any pattern you prefer. Spoon a few blocks of jelly on the cake and on the serving plate or cake stand. To give this cake a more festive look, sprinkle gold dragées on the cake.
11. Serve candied pecan nuts with each slice of cake.
12. The traditional custard and jelly are perishable items; therefore keep the cake refrigerated in an airtight container.

Quick and easy version

- Do not use coating but let the filling show. Spread whipped cream on top of the cake.
- Omit the decorative border around the cake.

Cupcakes

1. Bake cupcakes using the recipe for plain butter cake (p. 114) or plain chocolate mud cake (p. 112).
2. Cut a small hole into the top of each cupcake using an apple corer or a knife.
3. Brush each cupcake with sugar syrup and spoon or pipe traditional custard filling into each cupcake using a zip-lock or disposable piping bag.
4. Spread or pipe white chocolate ganache or buttercream coating on top of each cupcake.
5. Decorate with jelly cubes, glacé cherries and candied pecan nuts.

Butterscotch cake

The traditional South African malva pudding is transformed into a cake and instead of serving this dessert with custard on the side, the cake is filled with layers of condensed milk custard.

Makes 12-16 slices

Glacé icing decoration

Have the cake filled and coated, ready to be decorated.

- 65 g (½ cup/2¼ oz) icing (confectioner's) sugar
- 10 ml (2 t) water
- blue and green food colouring
- nonpareils (hundreds-and-thousands)

1. Stir together the icing sugar and water to make a thick glacé icing and divide it into two bowls.
2. Colour the icing in one bowl light green with a drop of green food colouring and the second bowl light blue with a drop of blue food colouring. Put a wet cloth over each bowl so that the icing does not dry out.
3. Pour each colour glacé icing into a zip-lock bag. Cut off a tip of each bag to make piping bags.
4. To pipe lines, touch the tip of the bag to the surface of the cake on one of the top edges. Slowly squeeze out icing while lifting the bag and moving the bag to the opposite edge of the cake. When nearing the opposite edge, lower the icing onto the surface of the cake and stop squeezing when you reach the edge. End the line by touching the tip of the bag to the surface of the cake.
5. Pipe thick diagonal lines or double lines in one direction over the top of the cake, alternating the colours, and then pipe diagonal lines over the first lines to the other side of the cake to make a criss-cross pattern.
6. Sprinkle nonpareils with a teaspoon in a thick line all along the top edge and around the bottom edge of the cake. If preferred, also stick nonpareils here and there on the sides of the cake.

Make the complete cake

- 2 round 20 cm (8 in) layers butterscotch cake (p. 124)
- 1 round serving plate or cake stand
- ½ batch condensed milk custard: traditional custard variation (p. 137)
- 1 batch meringue buttercream (p. 144) or traditional buttercream (p. 146)
- glacé icing decoration made according to directions
- nonpareils (hundreds and thousands)
- pastel-coloured sweets (optional)

Assembling and decorating the cake

1. Divide the cake layers and place the bottom cake layer on a serving plate or a cake stand.
2. Fill each of the cake layers with 125 ml (½ cup/4½ fl oz) of the traditional condensed milk custard filling before you stack the next one. Because the cake layers are thinner than usual, you need less filling.
3. Use 250 ml (1 cup/9 fl oz) of the buttercream coating and spread a thin layer all over the cake (see filling and coating cakes on p. 11). Spread the rest of the buttercream coating on top of the cake in an even layer but on the sides of the cake, use up and down movements with a palette knife to form a pattern.
4. Pipe criss-cross patterns of glacé icing on the cake as described above and decorate the top and bottom edge with nonpareils.
5. For a vintage appearance, arrange pastel-coloured sweets on top of the cake.
6. The condensed milk custard filling is a perishable item; therefore keep the cake refrigerated in an airtight container until 1 hour before serving.

Quick and easy version

- Do not use buttercream coating, rather make 1 full batch of condensed milk custard: traditional custard variation (p. 138) and use half to fill the cake and the other half to give the cake a thin coating.
- Omit the glacé icing decoration.

Cupcakes

1. Bake cupcakes using the butterscotch cake recipe (p. 124).
2. Cut a small hole into the top of each cupcake using an apple corer or a knife.
3. Spoon condensed milk custard filling: traditional custard variation into each cupcake.
4. Spread buttercream coating on top of each cupcake.
5. Decorate with criss-cross glacé piping, nonpareils and optional pastel-coloured sweets.

Peach melba cake

The traditional Peach Melba dessert consists of poached peaches, a fresh raspberry sauce and vanilla ice cream and is the inspiration for this dessert cake filled with delicious layers of peaches, white chocolate ganache and fresh raspberries and decorated with peach buttercream. If you cannot find raspberries, use fresh strawberries instead.

Makes 12-16 slices

Almond side decoration

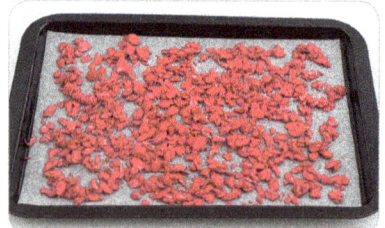

- 50 g (½ cup/1¾ oz) flaked almonds
- Red liquid food colouring

The cake should be freshly coated with buttercream and placed on a cooling rack, serving plate or cake stand.

1. Line a baking tray (sheet) with non-stick baking paper and pre-heat the oven to 100 °C (215 °F).
2. Mix 10 ml (2 t) red liquid food colouring with 250 ml (1 cup/9 fl oz) water.
3. Put the flaked almonds into the coloured water and leave to soak for 30 minutes.
4. Pour off the liquid through as sieve, dry the coloured almonds with kitchen towel and spread them out on the baking tray.
5. Dry the almonds in the oven for 20-25 minutes and leave to cool.
6. Decorate the bottom edge of the cake with coloured almonds.

Tip

The coloured almonds can be made up to two weeks in advance and kept in an airtight container. Make sure that the almonds are completely dry otherwise it will become mouldy.

Make the complete cake

- 2 round 20 cm (8 in) layers of butter cake (p. 114) or chocolate mud cake (p. 112) in the plain, raspberry or peach variation
- 1 round 20 cm (8 in) cake board or cardboard wrapped in foil or clingfilm or a round serving plate or cake stand
- 1 batch peach fruit preserve (p. 133) (I used canned peaches).
- ½ batch white chocolate ganache filling (p. 130)
- 125 g (1 cup/4½ oz) fresh raspberries (use more if you prefer)
- 1^{1}/$_{3}$ batches plain meringue buttercream (p. 144) or plain traditional buttercream (p. 146), coloured peach-orange (mix together yellow and red food colouring)
- almond side decoration as described
- 15-20 fresh raspberries
- 8-12 fresh or canned peach slices

Assembling and decorating the cake

1. Chop the peach fruit preserve into small pieces with a stick blender or food processor. Fold 180 ml (¾ cups/6¾ fl oz) into the white chocolate ganache filling to make your "peaches and ice cream" filling.

2. Set aside 125 ml (½ cup/4½ fl oz) of the peach fruit preserve to pour onto the top of the finished cake and fold the remaining 60 ml (¼ cup/2¼ fl oz) preserve into the buttercream.

3. Divide the cake layers and place the bottom cake layer on a board, serving plate or cake stand.

4. Pipe a circle around the edge of each cake layer with the peach buttercream to create a barrier for the filling, using 250 ml (1 cup/9 fl oz) in total for all three layers.

5. Fill each circle with 180 ml (¾ cup/6¾ fl oz) of the peach and ganache filling and put a few fresh raspberries on top of the filling before you stack the next one.

6. Coat the cake with the remaining 750 ml (3 cups/27 fl oz) of peach buttercream. (See filling and coating cakes p. 11.)

7. Spoon a few tablespoons of almonds at a time in your hand and press them all around the bottom edge of the cake, about ⅓ up the sides of the cake.

8. Spread the reserved 125 ml (½ cup/4½ fl oz) of peach fruit preserve on top of the cake. Arrange fresh or canned peach slices and fresh raspberries on the cake. Sprinkle some of the remaining coloured almonds on the cake.
9. The fresh raspberries and peach fruit preserve are perishable items; therefore keep the cake refrigerated in an airtight container until 1 hour before serving.

Quick and easy version

- Omit the coating and spread the filling more thinly to have some left over to spread on top of the cake.
- Omit the almond side decoration.

Cupcakes

1. Bake plain cupcakes using the recipe for butter cake (p. 114) or chocolate mud cake (p. 112).
2. Cut a small hole into the top of each cupcake using an apple corer or a knife.
3. Spoon or pipe peach and white chocolate ganache filling into each cupcake using a zip-lock or disposable piping bag.
4. Spread the top of each cupcake with peach buttercream.
5. Decorate with sliced peaches, fresh raspberries and coloured almonds.

Nougat cake

Light and fluffy layers of meringue frosting mixed with toasted nuts and glacé or dried fruit fill this dessert cake. It is inspired by homemade nougat which has a softer texture than purchased nougat.

Makes 12-16 slices

Fruit and nut snaps

Makes 48 snaps of 5 cm (2 in) in diameter baked in a normal muffin pan or 96 mini snaps of 3 cm (1¼ in) in diameter baked in a mini muffin pan

You will need 20 muffin-sized snaps or 30 mini muffin-sized snaps to go around a 20 cm (8 in) cake

- ✓ 60 g (¼ cup/2 oz) salted butter or baking margarine
- ✓ 50 g (¼ cup/1¾ oz) white sugar
- ✓ 30 ml (2 T) golden syrup (light corn syrup) or honey
- ✓ 60 g (½ cup/2 oz) cake flour
- ✓ 125 ml (½ cup/4½ fl oz) mixed nuts and glacé or dried fruits (I used 60 ml (¼ cup/2¼ fl oz) flaked almonds, 5 chopped dried Turkish apricots, 5 red and 5 green chopped glacé cherries)
- ✓ Small silver dragées (optional)

1. Preheat the oven to 180 °C (360 °F) for a conventional oven or 160 °C (320 °F) for a fan-assisted oven.
2. Spray normal muffin tins or mini muffin tins with non-stick cooking spray. Line a baking tray (sheet) with non-stick baking paper.
3. Assemble your ingredients.
4. Melt the butter, sugar and syrup or honey in a pot on the stove at medium heat. Heat and stir until all the sugar has dissolved.
5. Let the mixture cool slightly and then stir in the cake flour.
6. Drop 2.5-5 ml (½-1 t) of the mixture in each normal-sized muffin hole or 1.25 ml (¼ t) of the mixture in each mini muffin hole. The mixture spreads a lot, so do not use more mixture than suggested since this will give you very thick snaps.

7. Press some of the fruit and nut mixture on top of the batter in each muffin hole and sprinkle optional silver dragées on top.
8. Bake muffin-sized fruit and nut snaps for 8-10 minutes or bake mini muffin-sized snaps for 5-7 minutes. Remove the muffin trays from the oven and let the snaps cool for a few minutes to harden slightly.
9. Loosen the snaps with a knife and then flip over each muffin tray onto the lined baking tray so that the snaps can fall out. Turn over the snaps on the tray so that the fruit and nut mixture is on top again. Leave to cool.
10. Bake more fruit and nut snaps until the mixture has all been used.
11. Decorate the sides of the cake with the fruit and nut snaps.

Tip

The fruit and nut snaps can be made up to one week in advance and stored in an airtight container in a cool dark cupboard.

Make the complete cake

- ✓ 2 round 20 cm (8 in) layers of butter cake: chocolate variation (p. 115) or chocolate fudge cake (p. 120)
- ✓ 1 Round serving plate or cake stand
- ✓ 2 batches meringue buttercream: 7-minute meringue frosting variation (p. 145)
- ✓ 125 ml (½ cup/4½ fl oz) mixed nuts and glacé or dried fruits and/or chopped purchased nougat
- ✓ fruit and nut snaps made according to directions above
- ✓ extra mixed nuts and glacé or dried fruits and/or chopped purchased nougat for decoration
- ✓ candy floss (optional)
- ✓ silver dragées (optional)

Assembling and decorating the cake

1. Make 2 batches of 7-minute meringue frosting leaving the butter out of the recipe. Divide the frosting into two bowls and stir 125 ml (½ cup/4½ fl oz) fruit and nut mixture into one of the bowls to make a nougat filling.
2. Divide the cake layers and place the bottom cake layer on a serving plate or a cake stand.
3. Fill each of the cake layers with 310 ml (1¼ cups/11¼ fl oz) of the nougat filling before you stack the next one.

4. Coat the cake with one thick layer of 7-minute meringue frosting from the remaining bowl using your palette knife to create an uneven coating. Put big blobs of frosting on top of the cake, spreading it over onto the sides of the cake so that you do not get chocolate cake crumbs in the frosting. (See filling and coating cakes p. 11.) You could also dip your palette knife into boiled water to spread the frosting more easily.
5. Make the fruit and nut snaps as described above.
6. Press one row of fruit and nut snaps around the bottom edge of the cake and arrange another snap above every second fruit and nut snap.
7. Decorate the top of the cake with mixed nuts and fruits and/or chopped nougat. If preferred, arrange candy floss on top of the cake in the shape of a nest and sprinkle silver dragées on the cake if you wish.
8. Serve each slice of cake with extra fruit and nut snaps.

Note: 7-Minute meringue frosting does not keep well. The cake should be kept in an airtight container and eaten within two days. The frosting will still be edible after a few days but the appearance and texture of the frosting will change. If you prefer to keep the cake for a few days, rather use meringue buttercream to fill and coat the cake.

Quick and easy version

If you do not have time to make fruit and nut snaps, decorate this cake with nougat cut into strips and arranged around the cake.

Cupcakes

1. Bake cupcakes using the recipe for butter cake: chocolate variation (p. 115) or chocolate fudge cake (p. 120).
2. Spoon or pipe 7-minute meringue frosting onto each cupcake.
3. Decorate with a small fruit and nut snap, chopped purchased nougat and chopped glacé fruit or nuts.

Chai tea cake

This dessert cake is filled with tea-infused layers of creamy buttercream and decorated with spiced nuts.

Makes 8-12 slices

Spiced nuts

Use purchased spiced nuts or make your own.

- ✓ 105 g (¾ cup/3¾ oz) pistachios
- ✓ 105 g (¾ cup/3¾ oz) mixed nuts
- ✓ 60 g (4 T/2 oz) salted butter
- ✓ 2.5 ml (½ t) each cinnamon powder and mixed spice

Put the nuts into two separate microwave-safe bowls. Add 30 g (2 T/1 oz) salted butter together with 1.25 ml (¼ t) each cinnamon powder and mixed spice to each bowl. Microwave each bowl separately on high for 3-4 minutes, stirring at 1-minute intervals. Let the nuts cool down before using them on the cake.

Tip

You can make your spiced nuts up to two weeks in advance. Store them in an airtight container.

Decorative cake collar

- ✓ spiced nuts as above, of which 70 g (½ cup/2½ oz) pistachios and 70 g (½ cup/2½ oz) mixed nuts have been separately chopped into small pieces with a food processor or knife and the rest kept whole to decorate the cake.
- ✓ non-stick baking paper cut into a template to use as a guide for spreading the chopped nuts to the exact size of the cake
- ✓ chai cake, filled and only the sides coated (see steps 1-4 on page 101)

1. Cut a template for the collar from non-stick baking paper as wide and long as the cake, e.g. 10 x 50 cm (4 x 20 in). Place the template on your work bench.
2. Pour the chopped pistachios and the chopped mixed nuts in two distinct parallel lines along the length of the paper template, covering the entire surface of the paper.
3. Hold the cake in both hands and carefully roll the sides in the nuts, lifting the cake if necessary until the sides are completely covered.

Caramel circles

✓ 50 g (¼ cup/1¾ oz) castor sugar

1. Line a baking tray (sheet) with non-stick baking paper and spray with non-stick cooking spray.
2. Make a dry caramel with the sugar by heating the sugar in a pan on the stove at medium heat. Slowly stir the caramel with a wooden spoon while the sugar is melting to make sure that all the sugar crystals dissolve.
3. Immediately take the caramel off the heat when it turns an amber colour and all the sugar has melted.
4. Be very careful when working with caramel as it is very hot and can burn your fingers! Keep a bowl of ice water nearby to dip your hand into in case you are splashed with hot caramel.
5. Make caramel circles by swirling teaspoonful of caramel over the non-stick baking paper in circular patterns. Sprinkle leftover chopped spiced nuts on the caramel circles before they set.
6. Reserve the caramel circles to decorate the cake.

Tip

The caramel circles will keep for up to one week stored between layers of non-stick baking paper in an airtight container. Arrange them on the cake as close to serving as possible.

Make the complete cake

✓ 2 round 15 cm (6 in) layers of butter cake: chai tea variation (p. 115) or chocolate mud cake: chai tea variation (p. 113)
✓ 1 round serving plate or cake stand
✓ 1 batch traditional buttercream: chocolate tea or chai tea variation (p. 147)

Note: You could fill this cake with ½ batch condensed milk custard filling: tea variation or traditional custard filling: tea variation but the cake layers might slide apart if you try to roll the cake in nuts. Rather press the nuts against the cake with your hand as with the almond decoration on the Peach Melba cake on p. 90.

- ✓ decorative cake collar (see p. 98)
- ✓ caramel circles

Assembling and decorating the cake

1. Divide the cake layers and place the bottom cake layer on a piece of non-stick bakingpaper on a dinner plate.
2. Fill each cake layer with 125 ml (½ cup/4½ fl oz) of the chocolate tea or chai tea traditional buttercream before you stack the next one. (See filling and coating cakes p. 11.)
3. Put the cake in the refrigerator for 30 minutes for the cake to firm up so that it is easier to roll the cake.
4. Coat the sides of the cake with buttercream.
5. Decorate the sides of the cake with a decorative collar made from chopped spiced nuts as described.
6. Place the cake on a serving plate or cake stand and spread the remaining buttercream on top of the cake.
7. Decorate the cake with whole spiced nuts and caramel circles. Add the caramel circles just before serving.

Quick and easy version

- Omit the spiced nuts side decoration. If you do not have time to make caramel circles, decorate this cake with whole spiced nuts only.
- Use flaked almonds, chocolate vermicelli (sprinkles), nonpareils (hundreds-and-thousands), praline, peanut brittle, chocolate shavings, cake crumbs or cookie crumbs instead of spiced nuts.

Cupcakes

1. Bake cupcakes from the recipe for butter cake: chai tea variation (p. 115) or chocolate mud cake: chai tea variation (p. 113).
2. Pipe traditional buttercream: chocolate tea or chai tea variation (p. 147) onto each cupcake using a zip-lock bag or disposable piping bag.
3. Decorate with spiced nuts and caramel circles.

Pavlova cake

The meringue layers of a traditional pavlova are stacked with layers of vanilla cake and filled with creamy milk chocolate ganache.

Makes 12-16 slices

Cut-out hearts

- ✓ 60 g (2 oz) purchased almond paste (marzipan) or fondant icing (sugar paste/ready-to-roll icing)
- ✓ small heart cutter or any cookie cutter of your choice
- ✓ red or pink food colouring

1. Knead a few drops of food colouring into the almond paste or fondant icing.
2. Sprinkle icing (confectioner's) sugar on your work bench and roll out the almond paste or fondant icing to about 3 mm (1/8 in) thick.
3. Cut out heart shapes and set them aside to dry out slightly.

Tip

The heart shapes can be made up to two weeks in advance and stored in an airtight container in a cool dark cupboard. You could use pre-coloured pink fondant icing instead of colouring it yourself.

Make the complete cake

- ✓ 2 round 20 cm (8 in) meringue discs coloured light pink made from 2 batches of meringue mixture (pp. 153 and 155)
- ✓ 1 round 20 cm (8 in) layer plain butter cake (p. 114) or plain chocolate mud cake (p. 112)
- ✓ 1 round serving plate or cake stand
- ✓ 1 batch milk chocolate ganache filling (p. 130)
- ✓ cut-out hearts
- ✓ Fresh red rose petals (optional)

Assembling and decorating the cake

1. Make the meringue discs as described on pp. 153 and 155 and divide the cake into two layers.
2. Put a dollop of milk chocolate ganache filling on a serving plate or cake stand and place a cake layer on top.
3. Spread 180 ml (¾ cup/6¾ fl oz) of the milk chocolate ganache filling on each layer as you stack the cake, starting with the bottom cake layer.
4. Place a meringue disc on top of the filling and spread the same amount of milk chocolate ganache filling on the disc.
5. Place the second cake layer on the filling, spread filling on the cake layer and place the last meringue disc on top.
6. Spoon the remaining 180 ml (¾ cup/6¾ fl oz) of milk chocolate ganache into a zip-lock bag or disposable piping bag and snip off the tip of the bag. Pipe small blobs of ganache on top of the last meringue disc.
7. Decorate the meringue cake with pink cut-out hearts and optional fresh red rose petals.

Quick and easy version

- Use store-bought meringue discs instead of making your own. Use whipped cream and fresh fruit such as strawberries instead of ganache filling.
- Decorate the cake with purchased heart sweets instead of making fondant hearts.

Mini cakes

1. Bake mini meringue discs (pp. 153 and 155).
2. Stack two to three mini meringue discs with milk chocolate ganache filling in between.
3. Decorate each meringue stack with optional ribbon, pink cut-out hearts and optional rose petals.

Mint choc-chip cake

Mint choc-chip ice cream and mint-filled chocolates are the inspiration for this cake. The traditional flavour combination of mint and chocolate works very well in this dessert cake filled with layers of chocolate buttercream and decorated with a shiny chocolate glaze.

Makes 8-12 slices

Marbled and dotted glaze

Your cake should be filled, cut and coated before proceeding with these steps.

- ✓ ½ batch of white chocolate glaze (p. 151)
- ✓ 10 ml (2 t) cocoa powder
- ✓ a few drops of green food colouring
- ✓ peppermint essence (optional)

1. Make the white chocolate glaze according to the instructions on p. 151.
2. Scoop out 30 ml (2 T) of the glaze and mix with 10 ml (2 t) cocoa powder to make dark chocolate glaze.
3. Add a few drops of green food colouring and optional peppermint essence to the rest of the white chocolate glaze.
4. Put 15 ml (1 T) dark chocolate glaze and 15 ml (1 T) green glaze into two separate small zip-lock bags and set aside to use later.
5. If the remaining green glaze has set too much or you have left it overnight to set and it is too firm to pour, reheat in a microwave oven at 20% power or on the defrost-setting until it is runny enough to pour over the cake. It should have the consistency of thin custard. Stir gently so that you do not incorporate too many air bubbles into the glaze.
6. Reheat the remaining dark chocolate glaze for a few seconds in a microwave oven and pour it into the green glaze. The mixture will marble when it is poured onto the cake.
7. Place the slightly chilled, coated cake on a cooling rack over a baking tray (sheet) and pour the marbled glaze over the cake, preferably through a sieve, starting from the outer edge of the cake covering all the sides and the top of the cake with marbled glaze.
8. If the glaze in the zip-lock bags has set, heat the bags in a microwave oven at 50% power for 10 seconds at a time until the glaze is runny. Cut a small opening in the tip of each small zip-lock bag to make piping bags.

9. Pipe differently sized dark chocolate dots on top of the cake and pipe green dots into the dark dots. If the glaze on top of the cake is still moving slightly when piping the dots, some of the dots may distort, enhancing the abstract look of the cake.
10. Scrape the leftover glaze from the baking tray back into a container to reuse for another cake.
11. Carefully lift the cake from the cooling rack with an egg lifter, placing your other hand underneath the cake board, and slide the cake onto a serving plate or cake stand. Put the cake in the refrigerator for 20-30 minutes or leave for a few hours at room temperature for the glaze to set.

Tip

The chocolate glaze can be refrigerated in an airtight container for up to one month or frozen for six months. Bring back to room temperature before use. If you prefer, use only green glaze instead of marbling it.

Make the complete cake

- ✓ 2 round 15 cm (6 in) layers of butter cake: mint choc-chip variation (p. 115)
- ✓ 1 round 15 cm (6 in) cake board or cardboard wrapped in foil or clingfilm
- ✓ 1 round serving plate or cake stand
- ✓ 45 ml (3 T) mint-flavoured sugar syrup (p. 129) or mint liqueur
- ✓ 1 batch traditional buttercream (p. 146)
- ✓ 30 ml (2 T) divided cocoa powder
- ✓ 30 ml (2 T) cooled boiled water
- ✓ green food colouring
- ✓ mint essence
- ✓ marbled and dotted chocolate glaze as described
- ✓ fresh mint leaves
- ✓ ribbon 50 cm (20 in) and double-sided adhesive tape (optional)

Note: You could use ½ batch dark chocolate ganache filling: peppermint variation (p. 131) and ½ batch white chocolate ganache coating (p. 149) instead of 1 batch traditional buttercream.

Assembling and decorating the cake

1. Use half the traditional buttercream to make chocolate buttercream by adding together and mixing the water and cocoa powder before adding the mixture to the buttercream. Use the other half to make mint buttercream by adding a few drops of green food colouring and optional mint essence and mixing well.

1. Divide the cake layers and place the bottom cake layer on the board.
2. Brush each layer with the mint-flavoured sugar syrup before you fill it and stack the next one.
3. Fill each cake layer with 125 ml (½ cup/4½ fl oz) of the chocolate buttercream.
4. Coat the top and sides of the cake with mint buttercream (see filling and coating cakes p. 11).
5. Put the cake in the refrigerator for 15 minutes to set.
6. Decorate the cake with marbled and dotted glaze as described above.
7. Carefully lift the cake from the cooling rack with an egg lifter, placing your other hand underneath the cake and slide the cake onto a serving plate or cake stand with the egg lifter.
8. After the glaze has set, fasten a ribbon around the bottom of the cake and attach the ends with double-sided adhesive tape if preferred.
9. Arrange mint leaves on top of the cake.
10. The cake can be kept at room temperature or refrigerated in an airtight container until 1 hour before serving.

Quick and easy version

- Omit the mint-flavoured sugar syrup if you prefer.
- Leave out the marbled and dotted chocolate glaze.

Cupcakes

1. Bake cupcakes using the recipe for butter cake: mint choc-chip variation (p. 114).
2. Cut a small hole into the top of each cupcake using an apple corer or a knife.
3. Brush each cupcake with mint-flavoured sugar syrup and spoon or pipe chocolate buttercream into each cupcake using a zip-lock or disposable piping bag.
4. Dip the top of each cupcake into green chocolate glaze or pour it onto each cupcake with a teaspoon.
5. Pipe glaze dots on top of each cupcake and arrange fresh mint leaves on top.

Basic cakes

Before you start baking

How to line your baking tin:

1. Measure the circumference and height of the cake tins.
2. Cut a strip of non-stick baking paper for each tin, measuring 2.5 cm (1 in) more than the height of the tin and slightly longer than the circumference, to overlap when fitting into the tin. I always use 7.5 cm (3 in) deep cake tins but if your tins are shallower, extend the non-stick baking paper by 5 cm (2 in) more than the height of the tins.

Note: Use greaseproof or non-stick baking paper, not wax paper (sandwich wrap).

3. Fold over 2.5 cm (1 in) on one long edge of each strip and cut this flap at regular intervals. The cuts make the paper fit more easily.
4. Trace the tin bottoms onto non-stick baking paper and cut out.
5. Place the paper strips inside the tins with the cut flap eased on the bottom and place the bottom pieces on top of the flap to fit snugly and fully line the tins.
6. Spray the paper with non-stick cooking spray.
7. Follow these instructions for round or square tins.

Adjusting recipes

The cake recipes all give metric, imperial and cup measurements; stick to the same unit of measurement when measuring out your ingredients.

The standard cake recipes in this book all give enough cake batter for:

- Two 20 cm (8 in) round cake layers each 4-5 cm (1¾-2 in) high
- or two 17.5 cm (7 in) square cake layers each 4-5 cm (1¾-2 in) high
- or 24-36 cupcakes

It is easy to adjust the basic cake recipes by the following amounts for differently sized cake tins. Also remember: when making the cake variations, adjust the recipe according to cake size.

Metric and imperial

Round tins (2)	15 cm (6 in)	17.5 cm (7 in)	20 cm (8 in)	22 cm (9 in)	25 cm (10 in)	28 cm (11 in)	30 cm (12 in)	35 cm (14 in)
Square tins (2)	12 cm (5 in)	15 cm (6 in)	17.5 cm (7 in)	20 cm (8 in)	22 cm (9 in)	25 cm (10 in)	28 cm (11 in)	30 cm (12 in)
Recipe amount	½	¾	1	1¼	1½	2	2½	3

Of course you have to adjust the baking time as well. Bake larger cakes for a longer time and smaller cakes for a shorter time:

- For each 5 cm (2 in) difference in tin size, bake 10 minutes longer or shorter.

Chocolate mud cake

This is a moist cake with a dense, fudgy texture and is quite sweet. This cake is sturdy and will hold very well underneath a coating of ganache or buttercream. Bake this cake up to a week in advance of time, wrap in clingfilm and it will stay fresh until required. This recipe makes two 20 cm (8 in) round cake layers each 4 cm (1¾ in) high or two 17.5 cm (7 in) square cake layers each 4 cm (1¾ in) high or 36 cupcakes.

For other sizes, consult the table in 'Adjusting recipes' on p. 111.

- ✓ 220 g (1²⁄₃ cups/7¾ oz) white chocolate, broken into pieces
- ✓ 380 g (1²⁄₃ cups/13½ oz) salted butter or baking margarine
- ✓ 600 g (3 cups/1 lb 5¼ oz) white sugar
- ✓ 310 ml (1¼ cups/11¼ fl oz) full cream milk
- ✓ 450 g (3¾ cups/1 lb) cake flour
- ✓ 5 ml (1 t) baking powder
- ✓ 4 large eggs, lightly beaten
- ✓ 5 ml (1 t) vanilla essence

1. Preheat the oven to 160 °C (325 °F) for a conventional oven or 150 °C (300 °F) for a fan-assisted oven.
2. Line the base and sides of two 20 cm (8 in) round cake tins with non-stick baking paper and spray with non-stick cooking spray (see instructions on p. 110: 'Before you start baking').
3. Assemble your ingredients.
4. Mix the chocolate, butter, sugar and milk together in a bowl and heat in the microwave oven at 100% power. Stir well at 2-minute intervals until the mixture is melted and smooth. Let the mixture cool for 20 minutes.
5. Sift the flour and baking powder together and whisk the lightly beaten eggs, vanilla essence and the cooled chocolate mixture into the flour mixture with a balloon whisk or handheld electric beater.
6. Pour equal amounts of batter into the two lined tins and bake for about 1 hour and 30 minutes or until an inserted skewer comes out clean. If you prefer, place a piece of foil with the shiny side up over the top of each cake after 1 hour of baking so that the top of the cake does not over-brown and form an overly crunchy layer.
7. Take the cakes out of the oven and leave the foil on top so that the steam that forms can soften the crust slightly.
8. Let the cakes cool in the tins, preferably overnight. However, if you are pressed for time, let the cakes cool in the tins for 15 minutes after baking and then put the

tins with the cakes in the freezer for at least 30 minutes. This will cool and firm the cakes quickly so that you can fill and coat them immediately.

9. Turn the cakes out of the tins and tear off the non-stick baking paper.
10. Cut off the slightly crunchy layer on top to flatten the cake and divide each cake into two layers. (See instructions on p. 11: 'Filling and coating cakes'.)
11. Spread three of the layers with filling as you stack the layers on top of one another and cover the top and sides of the cake with buttercream or ganache coating.

Variations

- **Dark or milk chocolate:** Replace the white chocolate with dark or milk chocolate. Substitute 90 g (¾ cup/3¼ oz) cake flour with 80 g (¾ cup/2¾ oz) unsweetened cocoa powder. Add 15 ml (1 T) instant coffee granules to the milk and chocolate before heating.
- **Almond:** Replace 120 g (1 cup/4¼ oz) of the cake flour with ground almonds and replace the vanilla essence with 5 ml (1 t) almond essence.
- **Coconut:** Add 40 g (½ cup/1½ oz) toasted unsweetened desiccated coconut to the cake batter and replace the vanilla essence with 5 ml (1 t) coconut essence or coconut liqueur if you prefer.
- **Raspberry or berry:** Add 140 g (1 cup/5 oz) frozen raspberries or any other frozen berries lightly dusted with flour by dropping them into the batter after it has been divided into two cake tins. Push some of the berries down towards the bottom of the tins.
- **Caramel:** Use dark brown sugar instead of white sugar and replace the vanilla essence with 5 ml (1 t) caramel essence.
- **Chai tea:** Warm the milk and add 1 tea bag (any tea) to the warmed milk. Let it steep until the tea has infused into the milk. Remove the tea bag before heating the milk with the chocolate, butter and sugar. Add 2.5 ml (½ t) each of ginger powder, cinnamon powder and finely ground cardamom or mixed spice to the mixture.
- **Orange:** Add the grated zest of an orange to the batter. Use the juice of the orange with the milk to make up the liquid amount to 310 ml (1¼ cups/11¼ fl oz). If preferred, replace the vanilla essence with 5 ml (1 t) orange essence or orange blossom water.
- **Lemon or lime:** Add the grated zest of a lemon or lime to the batter. Use the juice of the lemon or lime with the milk to make up the liquid amount to 310 ml (1¼ cups/11¼ fl oz). If preferred, replace the vanilla essence with 5 ml (1 t) lemon essence.
- **Coffee:** Mix 30 ml (2 T) instant coffee granules with the milk before adding it to the chocolate, butter and sugar to be melted. Use light or dark brown sugar instead of white sugar.
- **Gluten-free:** Replace the cake flour with gluten-free baking flour.
- **Cupcakes:** Pour an ice cream scoopful (60 ml/¼ cup/ 2¼ fl oz) of batter into 36 muffin cases and bake in a conventional oven at 160 °C (325 °F) for 18-20 minutes or until an inserted skewer comes out clean.

Tip

A filled chocolate mud cake with a non-perishable filling will keep for six days at room temperature or eight days in the refrigerator. It can also be frozen filled or unfilled for up to three months.

Butter cake

This is a moist, buttery cake with a rich flavour. The cake is dense enough to hold up well under a coating of ganache or buttercream. This recipe makes two 20 cm (8 in) round cake layers each 4-5 cm (1¾-2 in) high or two 17.5 cm (7 in) square cake layers each 4-5 cm (1¾-2 in) high or 36 cupcakes.

For other sizes, consult the table in 'Adjusting recipes' on p. 111.

- 360 g (3 cups/12¾ oz) self-raising flour
- 350 g (1¾ cup/12½ oz) white sugar
- 350 g (1½ cups/12½ oz) salted butter or baking margarine, softened (or at room temperature)
- 6 large eggs
- 80 ml (⅓ cup/3 fl oz) milk
- 10 ml (2 t) vanilla essence

1. Preheat the oven to 160 °C (325 °F) for a conventional oven or 150 °C (300 °F) for a fan-assisted oven.
2. Line the base and sides of two 20 cm (8 in) round cake tins with non-stick baking paper and spray with non-stick cooking spray (see instructions on p. 110: 'Before you start baking').
3. Assemble your ingredients.
4. Sift the flour into a mixing bowl and add the sugar, softened butter and eggs. Mix for 30 seconds with a handheld electric beater or a standing mixer on medium speed.
5. Add the milk and vanilla essence and beat for another 1 minute and 30 seconds or until the mixture looks light and fluffy.
6. Spoon equal amounts of batter into the lined cake tins and bake for about 50 minutes or until an inserted skewer comes out clean.
7. Let the cakes cool in the tins, preferably overnight. However, if you are pressed for time, let the cakes cool in the tins for 15 minutes after baking and then put the tins with the cakes in the freezer for at least 30 minutes. This will cool and firm the cakes quickly so that you can fill and coat them immediately.
8. Turn the cakes out of the tins and tear off the non-stick baking paper.
9. Divide each cake into two layers. (See instructions for filling and coating cakes on p. 11.)
10. Spread three of the layers with filling as you stack the layers on top of one another and cover the top and sides of the cake with buttercream or ganache coating.

Variations

- **Strawberry:** Mix 125 ml (½ cup/4½ fl oz) chunky strawberry jam into the cake batter. You could also add a few drops of red food colouring and strawberry essence instead of vanilla essence to the batter.
- **Chocolate:** To make a chocolate cake, substitute 60 g (½ cup/2 oz) flour with 50 g (½ cup/1¾ oz) of unsweetened cocoa powder. Add 5 ml (1 t) instant coffee granules to the milk to give the cake a deeper flavour.
- **Coffee:** Stir 30 ml (2 T) instant coffee granules into the milk before adding it to the cake batter.
- **Caramel:** Use soft brown (treacle or demerara) sugar instead of white sugar and replace the vanilla essence with 10 ml (2 t) caramel essence.
- **Pineapple, apple, peach or pear:** Add 1 can (385 g/13¾ oz) of drained pineapple pieces, drained apple slices, drained and chopped peach or pear slices to the cake batter, folding them in before spooning the batter into the cake tins.
- **Almond:** Add 35 g (¼ cup/1¼ oz) ground almonds to the cake batter and replace 5 ml (1 t) of the vanilla essence with 5 ml (1 t) almond essence.
- **Coconut:** Add 70 g (½ cup/2½ oz) toasted desiccated coconut to the cake batter and replace 5 ml (1 t) of the vanilla essence with 5 ml (1 t) coconut essence or coconut liqueur if preferred.
- **Passionfruit:** Replace the 80 ml (⅓ cup/3 fl oz) milk with passionfruit juice or with 1 small can (115 g/4 oz) or 125 ml (½ cup/4½ fl oz) passionfruit pulp with or without seeds.
- **Chai tea:** Replace the milk with 80 ml (⅓ cup/3 fl oz) cooled milky tea and add 2.5 ml (½ t) each of ginger powder, cinnamon powder and finely ground cardamom or mixed spice to the mixture.
- **Orange, lemon or lime:** Add the grated zest of 1 orange, lemon or lime to the cake batter and use the juice of the orange, lemon or lime with milk to make up the liquid amount to 80 ml (⅓ cup/3 fl oz).
- **Raspberry or berry:** Add 140 g (1 cup/5 oz) frozen raspberries or any other frozen berries lightly dusted with flour by dropping them into the batter after it has been divided into two cake tins. Push some of the berries down towards the bottom of the tins.
- **Mint choc-chip:** To make a mint choc-chip cake, replace the vanilla essence with 10 ml (2 t) mint essence and add a few drops of green food colouring to the cake mixture. Spray 150 g (1 cup/5¼ oz) chocolate chips with non-stick cooking spray and then coat them with a tablespoon of flour. Fold half of the chocolate chips into the finished batter and sprinkle the other half over the batter after it has been spooned into the tins. This will prevent them from sinking. If preferred, add 5 ml (1 t) chopped fresh mint to the batter.
- **Peanut butter:** Mix 125 ml (½ cup/4½ fl oz) chunky peanut butter into the cake batter.
- **Gluten-free:** Replace the self-raising cake flour with self-raising gluten-free flour.
- **Cupcakes:** Pour an ice cream scoopful (60 ml/¼ cup/ 2¼ fl oz) of batter into 36 muffin cases and bake in a conventional oven at 160 °C (325 °F) for 18-20 minutes or until an inserted skewer or toothpick comes out clean.

Tip

A filled butter cake with a non-perishable filling will keep for five days at room temperature or seven days in the refrigerator. It can also be frozen filled or unfilled for up to three months.

Apple crumble cake

The crumble layer on top of this moist, rich apple cake is buttery and crunchy and reminds you of apple tart. This recipe makes two 20 cm (8 in) round cake layers each 4 cm (1¾ in) high or two 17.5 cm (7 in) square cake layers each 4 cm (1¾ in) high or 24 cupcakes.

For other sizes, consult the table in 'Adjusting recipes' on p. 111.

Crumble

- ✓ 90 g (⅓ cup/3¼ oz) salted butter or baking margarine, at room temperature
- ✓ 45 ml (3 T) white sugar
- ✓ 20 g (¼ cup/¾ oz) unsweetened desiccated coconut (optional)
- ✓ 120 g (1 cup/4¼ oz) cake flour

Cake

- ✓ 240 g (2 cups/8½ oz) self-raising flour
- ✓ 250 g (1¼ cups/9 oz) white sugar
- ✓ 230 g (1 cup/8¼ oz) salted butter or baking margarine, softened (or at room temperature)
- ✓ 4 large eggs
- ✓ 20 ml (4 t) milk
- ✓ 5 ml (1 t) vanilla essence or cinnamon powder
- ✓ 400 g (2 cups/14¼ oz) peeled, chopped, cooked and cooled apples or a 385 g (13¾ oz) can of sliced apples, drained and chopped

1. Preheat the oven to 160 °C (325 °F) for a conventional oven or 150 °C (300 °F) for a fan-assisted oven.
2. Place two 50 x 2.5 cm (20 x 1 in) strips of non-stick baking paper crossways on the bottom of each round 20 cm (8 in) tin and then line the base and sides of the two cake tins and spray with non-stick cooking spray (see instructions on p. 110: 'Before you start baking').
3. Assemble your ingredients.
4. Make the crumble mixture by placing all the ingredients in a bowl and mixing well with a wooden spoon or beat the mixture with a standing mixer on a slow speed.
5. Press the mixture together to form a ball and wrap the ball with clingfilm.
6. Put the crumble dough into the freezer for 15 minutes.
7. Sift the flour into a mixing bowl and add the sugar, softened butter and eggs. Mix for 30 seconds with a handheld electric beater or standing mixer on medium speed.

8. Add the milk and vanilla essence and beat for another 1 minute and 30 seconds or until the mixture looks light and fluffy.
9. Fold the canned or cooked, cooled apples into the cake batter.
10. Spoon equal amounts of batter into the lined cake tins. Grate the crumble dough over the top of each cake and bake for 1 hour to 1 hour and 10 minutes or until an inserted skewer comes out clean and the crumble is golden brown on top.
11. Let the cakes cool in the tins.
12. Carefully lift each cake out of its tin, holding onto the rectangular strips and tear off the non-stick baking paper.
13. Divide the cake layers, spread filling in between the layers and place the cake on a serving plate.

Variations

- **Fruit:** Replace the apples with a 385 g (13¾ oz) can of drained pineapple pieces, drained berries, drained and chopped pears or drained and chopped peaches.
- **Cupcakes:** Pour an ice cream scoopful (60 ml/¼ cup/2¼ fl oz) of batter into 24 muffin cases and put two teaspoons of crumble mixture on top of each cupcake. Bake in a conventional oven at 160 °C (325 °F) for 20-25 minutes or until an inserted skewer comes out clean and the crumble is golden brown on top.

Tip

- A filled apple crumble cake with a non-perishable filling will keep for three days at room temperature or five days in the refrigerator.
- It can also be frozen filled or unfilled for up to three months.

Coconut meringue cake

Crunchy baked coconut meringue is the topping for this moist, buttery cake. This recipe makes two 20 cm (8 in) round cake layers each 4 cm (1¾ in) high or two 17.5 cm (7 in) square cake layers each 4 cm (1¾ in) high or 24 cupcakes.

For other sizes, consult the table in 'Adjusting recipes' on p. 111.

- ✓ 240 g (2 cups/8½ oz) self-raising flour
- ✓ 250 g (1¼ cups/9 oz) white sugar
- ✓ 230 g (1 cup/8¼ oz) salted butter or baking margarine, softened (or at room temperature)
- ✓ 2 large eggs, whole
- ✓ 4 large eggs, separated (keep yolks for the cake and whites for meringue)
- ✓ 60 ml (¼ cup/2¼ fl oz) milk
- ✓ 5 ml (1 t) vanilla essence

Topping

- ✓ 4 large egg whites (from separated eggs)
- ✓ 130 g (⅔ cup/4½ oz) white sugar
- ✓ 100 g (1¼ cup/3½ oz) unsweetened dessicated coconut
- ✓ 5 ml (1 t) vanilla essence

1. Preheat the oven to 160 °C (325 °F) for a conventional oven or 150 °C (300 °F) for a fan-assisted oven.
2. Place two 50 x 2.5 cm (20 x 1 in) strips of non-stick baking paper crossways on the bottom of each round 20 cm (8 in) tin and then line the base and sides of the two cake tins and spray with non-stick cooking spray (see instructions on p. 110: 'Before you start baking').
3. Assemble your ingredients.
4. Sift the flour into a mixing bowl and add the sugar, softened butter, 2 whole eggs and 4 egg yolks. Mix for 30 seconds with a handheld electric beater or standing mixer on medium speed.
5. Add the milk and vanilla essence and beat for another 1 minute and 30 seconds or until the mixture looks light and fluffy.
6. Spoon equal amounts of batter into the lined cake tins.

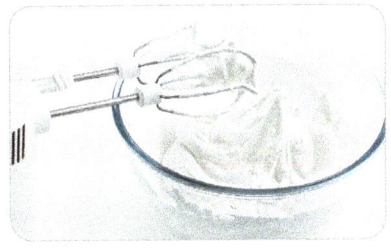 

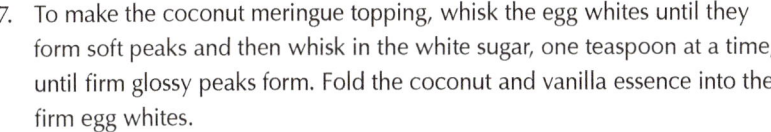

7. To make the coconut meringue topping, whisk the egg whites until they form soft peaks and then whisk in the white sugar, one teaspoon at a time, until firm glossy peaks form. Fold the coconut and vanilla essence into the firm egg whites.

8. Spoon the coconut meringue mixture equally over the top of each cake and bake for 1 hour or until the meringue is golden brown and an inserted skewer comes out clean.

9. Let the cakes cool in the tins.

10. Carefully lift each cake out of its tin, holding onto the rectangular strips and tear off the non-stick baking paper.

11. Spread filling in between the two cake layers or divide each cake and spread jam in between each layer. Place the cake on a serving plate.

Variations

- **Apricot or jam:** Spoon dollops of apricot jam or any jam of your choice on top of the cake batter in each tin. Use about 60 ml (¼ cup/2¼ fl oz) of jam in total. Then spoon the coconut meringue on top.
- **Fruit:** Fold a drained 385 g (13¾ oz) can of chopped apples, pineapple pieces, berries, chopped pears or chopped peaches into the finished cake batter. Spoon the coconut meringue on top of the batter.
- **Cupcakes:** Pour slightly less than an ice cream scoopful (45 ml/3 T) of batter into 24 muffin cases and spoon ½ a teaspoonful of apricot jam or any jam of your choice onto the batter. Put 1-2 heaped teaspoons of coconut meringue mixture on top of each cupcake. Bake in a conventional oven at 160 °C (325 °F) for 30-35 minutes or until an inserted skewer comes out clean and the meringue is golden brown on top.

Tip

A filled coconut meringue cake with a non-perishable filling will keep for five days at room temperature or seven days in the refrigerator. It can also be frozen filled or unfilled for up to three months.

Chocolate fudge cake

This sinfully rich and firm cake has a deep chocolaty taste. This recipe makes two 20 cm (8 in) round cake layers each 4 cm (1¾ in) high or two 17.5 cm (7 in) square cake layers each 4 cm (1¾ in) high or 36 cupcakes.

For other sizes, consult the table in 'Adjusting recipes' on p. 111.

- ✓ 230 g (1 cup/8¼ oz) salted butter or baking margarine at room temperature
- ✓ 400 g (2 cups/14¼ oz) white sugar
- ✓ 5 ml (1 t) instant coffee granules dissolved in 10 ml (2 t) water
- ✓ 4 large eggs
- ✓ 300 g (2½ cups/10¾ oz) cake flour
- ✓ 80 g (¾ cup/2¾ oz) cocoa powder
- ✓ 5 ml (1 t) baking powder
- ✓ 5 ml (1 t) bicarbonate of soda
- ✓ 250 ml (1 cup/9 fl oz) buttermilk

1. Preheat the oven to 160 °C (325 °F) for a conventional oven or 150 °C (300 °F) for a fan-assisted oven.
2. Line the base and sides of two 20 cm (8 in) round cake tins with non-stick baking paper and spray with non-stick cooking spray (see instructions on p. 110: 'Before you start baking').
3. Assemble your ingredients.
4. Using a handheld electric beater or a standing mixer, beat together the butter, sugar and coffee on medium speed until the mixture looks light and fluffy.
5. Add the eggs one at a time and mix well after each egg has been added.
6. Sift the cake flour, cocoa powder, baking powder and bicarbonate of soda together.
7. Add the flour mixture alternately with the buttermilk to the butter mixture and mix on a slow speed until all the ingredients have just been incorporated, starting and ending with flour. Do not over-mix as this can produce a chewy cake.

8. Spoon the batter into the lined tins and spread it evenly with a spatula.
9. Bake for about 50 minutes to 1 hour or until an inserted skewer or toothpick comes out clean.
10. Let the cakes cool in the tins, preferably overnight. However, if you are pressed for time, let the cakes cool in the tins for 15 minutes after baking and then put the tins with the cakes in the freezer for at least 30 minutes. This will cool and firm the cakes quickly so that you can fill and coat them immediately.
11. Turn the cakes out of the tins and tear off the non-stick baking paper.
12. Divide each cake into two layers. (See instructions for filling and coating cakes on p. 11.)
13. Spread three of the layers with filling as you stack the layers on top of one another and cover the top and sides of the cake with buttercream or ganache coating.

Variations

- **Hazelnut:** Mix 125 ml (½ cup/4½ fl oz) Nutella hazelnut spread into the cake batter.
- **Orange chocolate fudge cake:** Add the grated zest of 1 orange to the cake batter. Leave out the coffee and add 5 ml (1 t) orange essence or orange flower water to the batter if preferred.
- **Coconut:** Add 70 g (½ cup/2½ oz) toasted desiccated coconut to the cake batter and leave out the coffee. If preferred, add 5 ml (1 t) coconut essence or coconut liqueur to the batter.
- **Coffee:** Use 30 ml (2 T) instant coffee granules instead of 5 ml (1 t).
- **Cupcakes:** Use an ice-cream scoop to spoon equal amounts (60 ml/¼ cup/2¼ fl oz) of batter into 36 muffin cases and bake in a conventional oven at 160 °C (325 °F) for 18-20 minutes or until an inserted skewer or toothpick comes out clean.

Tip

A filled chocolate fudge cake with non-perishable filling will keep for six days at room temperature or eight days in the refrigerator. It can also be frozen filled or unfilled for up to three months.

Salted caramel cake

This moist, buttery cake has a wonderful caramel flavour. This recipe makes two 20 cm (8 in) round cake layers each 4-5 cm (1¾-2 in) high or two 17.5 cm (7 in) square cake layers each 4-5 cm (1¾-2 in) high or 36 cupcakes.

For other sizes, consult the table in 'Adjusting recipes' on p. 111.

- ✓ 230 g (1 cup/8¼ oz) salted butter or baking margarine at room temperature
- ✓ 400 g (2 cups/14¼ oz) brown treacle or demerara sugar
- ✓ 5 ml (1 t) vanilla or caramel essence
- ✓ 4 large eggs
- ✓ 390 g (3¼ cups/14 oz) self-raising flour
- ✓ 2.5 ml (½ t) fine table salt
- ✓ 250 ml (1 cup/9 fl oz) full cream milk

1. Preheat the oven to 160 °C (325 °F) for a conventional oven or 150 °C (300 °F) for a fan-assisted oven.
2. Line the base and sides of two 20 cm (8 in) round cake tins with non-stick baking paper and spray with non-stick cooking spray (see instructions on p. 110: 'Before you start baking').
3. Assemble your ingredients.
4. Using a handheld electric beater or a standing mixer, beat together the butter, brown sugar and vanilla or caramel essence on medium speed until the mixture looks light and fluffy.
5. Add the eggs one at a time and mix well after each egg has been added.
6. Sift the self-raising flour and salt together. Add a third of the flour mixture and half of the milk to the butter mixture and mix on a slow speed until all the ingredients have just been incorporated. Add another third of the flour mixture and the rest of the milk to the butter mixture, mix on a slow speed and lastly add the rest of the flour mixture, beating until all the ingredients have been incorporated. The mixture will be soft and might look slightly curdled.

7. Spoon the batter into the lined tins and spread it evenly with a spatula.
8. Bake for about 50 minutes to 1 hour or until an inserted skewer or toothpick comes out clean.
9. Let the cakes cool in the tins, preferably overnight. However, if you are pressed for time, let the cakes cool in the tins for 15 minutes after baking and then put the tins with the cakes in the freezer for at least 30 minutes. This will cool and firm the cakes quickly so that you can fill and coat them immediately.
10. Turn the cakes out of the tins and tear off the non-stick baking paper.
11. Divide each cake into two layers. (See instructions for filling and coating cakes on p. 11.)
12. Spread three of the layers with filling as you stack the layers on top of one another and cover the top and sides of the cake with buttercream or ganache coating.

Variation

- **Cupcakes:** Use an ice-cream scoop to spoon equal amounts (60 ml/¼ cup/2¼ fl oz) of batter into 36 muffin cases and bake in a conventional oven at 160 °C (325 °F) for 18-20 minutes or until an inserted skewer or toothpick comes out clean.

Tip

A filled caramel cake with a non-perishable filling will keep for six days at room temperature or eight days in the refrigerator. It can also be frozen filled or unfilled for up to three months.

Butterscotch cake

The unique flavour of a traditional South African malva pudding is found in this cake. The sponge is quite dry and needs to be moistened with syrup after baking. This recipe makes two 20 cm (8 in) round cake layers each 3.5 cm (1½ in) high or two 17.5 cm (7 in) square cake layers each 3.5 cm (1½ in) high or 24 cupcakes.

For other sizes, consult the table in 'Adjusting recipes' on p. 111.

- ✓ 30 g (2 T/1 oz) salted butter or baking margarine, melted
- ✓ 4 large eggs
- ✓ 400 g (2 cups/14¼ oz) white sugar
- ✓ 300 g (2½ cups/10¾ oz) cake flour
- ✓ 30 ml (2 T) smooth apricot jam
- ✓ 10 ml (2 t) bicarbonate of soda
- ✓ 250 ml (1 cup/9 fl oz) milk
- ✓ 10 ml (2 t) white vinegar
- ✓ 10 ml (2 t) vanilla or caramel essence

Sauce

- ✓ 125 ml (½ cup/4½ fl oz) milk
- ✓ 100 g (½ cup/3½ oz) soft brown treacle or demerara sugar
- ✓ 60 g (¼ cup/2 oz) salted butter or baking margarine
- ✓ 5 ml (1 t) vanilla or caramel essence
- ✓ 15 ml (1 T) brandy (optional)

1. Preheat the oven to 180 °C (360 °F) for a conventional oven or 160 °C (320 °F) for a fan-assisted oven.
2. Line the base and sides of two 20 cm (8 in) round cake tins with non-stick baking paper and spray with non-stick cooking spray (see instructions on p. 110: 'Before you start baking').
3. Melt the butter in a microwave oven and set aside to cool.
4. Beat the eggs and sugar with a handheld electric beater or a standing mixer with a whisk attachment until the eggs are thick and light yellow and add the cooled butter to the egg mixture.
5. Sift the flour into a bowl.
6. Mix the apricot jam with the bicarbonate of soda and stir in the milk, vinegar and vanilla or caramel essence.
7. Fold a third of the flour and half of the milk mixture into the egg mixture using a metal spoon or spatula. Add another third of the flour and the rest of the milk to the egg mixture. Lastly fold in the rest of the flour.

8. Pour equal amounts of batter into the lined cake tins. Place a piece of foil, shiny side up, tightly over each tin.
9. Bake for about 40 minutes and then remove the foil. Bake for another 5-10 minutes or until the top is golden brown or an inserted skewer comes out clean.
10. Make the sauce just before the cakes come out of the oven. Heat all the ingredients together in a pot on the stove at medium heat until the sugar has melted but do not boil. If preferred, add brandy after heating the syrup.
11. Prick the warm cakes with a skewer or toothpick and ladle the hot sauce over the cakes.
12. Let the cakes cool in the tins for at least 15 minutes and then put them in the refrigerator, preferably overnight or in the freezer for 30-60 minutes. This will make it easier to work with the cakes.
13. Turn the cakes out of the tins and tear off the non-stick baking paper.
14. Divide each cake into two layers. (See instructions for filling and coating cakes on p. 11.)
15. Spread three of the layers with filling as you stack the layers on top of one another and cover the top and sides of the cake with buttercream or ganache coating.

Variation

- **Cupcakes:** Use an ice-cream scoop to spoon equal amounts (60 ml/¼ cup/2¼ fl oz) of batter into 24 muffin cases and bake in a conventional oven at 180 °C (350 °F) for 25 minutes or until an inserted skewer or toothpick comes out clean. Pour 5-10 ml (1-2 t) warm sauce over the warm, pricked cupcakes.

Tip
A filled butterscotch cake will keep for four days in the refrigerator. It can also be frozen filled or unfilled for up to three months.

Almond sponge cake

This thin layer of almond cake (*joconde*) is very flexible and can be stacked as thin layers in a filled cake or used as a decorative outer layer for a cake. The recipe makes one 25 x 37.5 cm (10 x 15 in) baking tray (sheet) cake layer. (If you bake with a slightly smaller baking tray you will get a thicker sponge that might have to bake a few minutes longer. If you bake with a slightly larger baking tray your sponge will be thinner and you would have to bake it for a few minutes less.)

Decorative paste

- ✓ 35 g (3 T/1¼ oz) salted butter or baking margarine, at room temperature
- ✓ 35 g (¼ cup/1¼ oz) icing (confectioner's) sugar
- ✓ 1 large egg white, at room temperature
- ✓ 30 g (¼ cup/1 oz) cake flour
- ✓ 10 g (1½ T/⅓ oz) cornflour or cocoa powder
- ✓ Food colouring (optional)

Almond sponge

- ✓ 60 g (⅓ cup & 1 T/2 oz) ground almonds
- ✓ 60 g (½ cup/2 oz) icing (confectioner's) sugar
- ✓ 20 g (3 T/⅔ oz) cake flour
- ✓ 20 g (3 T/⅔ oz) cornflour (cornstarch) or cocoa powder
- ✓ 2 large eggs, whole, at room temperature
- ✓ 2 large egg whites only, at room temperature
- ✓ 10 g (1 T/⅓ oz) white sugar
- ✓ 10 g (2 t/⅓ oz) salted butter or baking margarine, melted
- ✓ Food colouring (optional)

1. Preheat the oven to 180 °C (350 °F) for a conventional oven or 160 °C (320 °F) for a fan-assisted oven.
2. Line the base of a 25 x 37.5 cm (10 x 15 in) baking tray (sheet) or jelly-roll pan with non-stick baking paper or with a Silpat® mat and spray with non-stick cooking spray.
3. Assemble your decorative paste ingredients.
4. Cream together the butter and icing sugar with a handheld electric beater or a standing mixer. Add the egg white and whisk until incorporated.
5. Whisk in the cake flour and the cornflour or cocoa powder until just combined.
6. Stir in optional food colouring. If you use a lot of food colouring, the mixture might look slightly curdled but this will not affect the end result.
7. Spread the decorative paste on the non-stick baking paper or over a stencil or spoon it into a zip-lock bag or disposable piping bag. Snip off the tip of the

bag and pipe decorative patterns on the non-stick baking paper. If you are unsure about piping decorative patterns, draw patterns in pencil on the back of the paper to guide you when piping.

8. Put the baking tray with the decorative patterns in a freezer for 20-30 minutes or until the paste is hard.

9. Assemble the ingredients for the almond sponge. To make the almond sponge, mix together the ground almonds, icing sugar, cake flour and cornflour or cocoa powder in a large bowl.

10. Whisk the whole eggs into the almond mixture one at a time using a handheld electric beater or a standing mixer. Make sure that the first egg is beaten in very well before adding the next egg. After both the eggs are added, beat for another 5 minutes on medium speed to aerate the mixture.

11. Whip the egg whites and sugar in a clean bowl with clean beaters until the egg whites are glossy and firm but not dry.

12. Fold the egg whites into the almond mixture and then fold in the cooled melted butter and optional food colouring.

13. Take the baking tray out of the freezer and pour the almond batter over the decorative patterns, tilting the tray for the mixture to spread evenly or spread it into a thin layer with an offset spatula. Tap the tray a few times so that the mixture spreads evenly and to burst some of the air bubbles.

14. Bake the almond sponge for about 7-8 minutes or until lightly golden brown on top.

15. Let the sponge cool for a few minutes and then invert it onto a piece of non-stick baking paper or clingfilm sprinkled with icing sugar.

16. Pull off the non-stick baking paper or Silpat® mat from the top of the sponge and trim off any crispy edges.

17. Cut the sponge into the desired size or into round discs to use as stacked layers.

Tip

Almond sponge layers will keep for four days at room temperature or six days in the refrigerator, wrapped in clingfilm, or the sponge layers can be frozen for up to three months.

Sugar syrup

Use plain sugar syrup or infused with different flavours such as vanilla, lemon rind, coffee or chocolate to enhance the taste and moistness of the cake. Brush it over the cake layers with a pastry brush or pour into a spray bottle and spray it on the cake layers. Too much sugar syrup can make a cake taste overly sweet so use restraint when brushing it on the cake layers. Makes 180 ml (¾ cups/6¾ fl oz).

Adjust the amount of syrup by consulting the table in 'Adjusting the recipe' on p. 129.

- 100 g (½ cup/3½ oz) white sugar
- 125 ml (½ cup/4½ fl oz) water

1. Put the sugar and water in a pot on the stove, stirring occasionally until all the sugar has dissolved and slowly bring to a boil.
2. Remove from the heat and let the syrup cool down to room temperature or refrigerate overnight.

Tip
The syrup can be kept in the refrigerator for up to 1 month.

Variations

- **Strawberry:** Mix 60 ml (¼ cup/2¼ fl oz) of chunky strawberry jam into the sugar syrup. You could also add 5 ml (1 t) strawberry essence to the boiled syrup.
- **Caramel:** Use soft brown (treacle or demerara) sugar instead of white sugar.
- **Mint:** Finely chop 15 ml (1 T) fresh mint leaves and put it into the syrup as it comes to a boil. Leave the chopped mint in the sugar syrup to infuse until the syrup is cool. Pour the syrup through a sieve to remove the leaves.
- **Almond:** Add 5 ml (1 t) almond essence or 15 ml (1 T) almond liqueur to the boiled syrup.
- **Vanilla:** Cut open 1 vanilla pod lengthwise and put it into the syrup as it comes to a boil. Leave the vanilla pod in the sugar syrup to infuse. If you do not have a vanilla pod, add 5 ml (1 t) vanilla essence to the boiled syrup.
- **Chocolate:** Add 30 ml (2 T) of unsweetened cocoa powder to the sugar and water mixture before bringing it to a boil.
- **Orange, lemon or lime:** Add the juice and grated zest of 1 orange, 1 lemon or 2 limes to the boiled syrup.
- **Passionfruit:** Mix 60 ml (¼ cup/2¼ fl oz) passionfruit pulp with or without seeds or passionfruit juice into the boiled syrup.
- **Coffee:** Add 15 ml (1 T) instant coffee granules to the sugar and water mixture before boiling.
- **Sherry or liqueur:** Add 60 ml (¼ cup/2¼ fl oz) sweet sherry or liqueur to the boiled mixture.

Adjusting the recipe

Adjust the basic recipe by the following amounts for differently sized cakes:

Round cake	15 cm (6 in)	17.5 cm (7 in)	20 cm (8 in)	22 cm (9 in)	25 cm (10 in)	30 cm (12 in)
Square cake	12 cm (5 in)	15 cm (6 in)	17.5 cm (7 in)	20 cm (8 in)	22 cm (9 in)	28 cm (11 in)
Recipe amount	¼	¼	⅓	½	⅔	1

Chocolate ganache filling

Ganache filling is soft and mousse-like with a rich, chocolate flavour. The quality of the flavour relies on the quality of the chocolate used. Makes 750 ml-1 ℓ (3-4 cups/27-36 fl oz).

Adjust the amount of filling by consulting the table in 'Adjusting the recipe' on p. 131.

- ✓ 400 g (3 cups/14¼ oz) dark chocolate, chopped or 560 g (4 cups/1 lb 4 oz) milk chocolate, chopped or 560 g (4 cups/1 lb 4 oz) white chocolate, chopped
- ✓ 375 ml (1½ cups/13½ fl oz) whipping cream

1. Assemble your ingredients.
2. Heat the chopped chocolate and cream together in a bowl in a microwave oven at 20% power or at the defrost setting. Stir at 2-minute intervals until the mixture is melted and smooth.
3. Refrigerate mixture until very cold or preferably overnight.
4. Beat mixture with a handheld electric beater until light and fluffy, but be careful not to overbeat as it can curdle.
5. Spread directly onto cake layers to sandwich the layers together.

Tip

- If your ganache has overheated, it will separate. Let the ganache cool down and come to almost room temperature, then quickly whip the expelled fat back into the chocolate mixture with a handheld whisk or electric beater until it has been incorporated. Leave the ganache to set and use normally.
- If the mixture curdles from whipping it for too long, repeat steps 2ß-3, reheating the mixture and then cooling it down again before beating it. The texture will be grainier and firmer than usual.
- The filling can be refrigerated in an airtight container for up to two weeks or frozen for six months. Bring back to room temperature before use.

Adjusting the recipe

The recipes for ganache filling are all for a 20 cm (8 in) round cake baked in two layers. However, adjust the basic recipe by the following amounts for differently sized cakes:

Round cake	15 cm (6 in)	17.5 cm (7 in)	20 cm (8 in)	22 cm (9 in)	25 cm (10 in)	30 cm (12 in)
Square cake	12 cm (5 in)	15 cm (6 in)	17.5 cm (7 in)	20 cm (8 in)	22 cm (9 in)	28 cm (11 in)
Recipe amount	¼–½	½–¾	¾–1	1–1¼	1¼–1½	1¾–2

Variations

- **Vanilla:** Add the seeds of 1 vanilla pod to the cream and chocolate before heating.
- **Strawberry:** Fold 60 ml (¼ cup/2¼ fl oz) chunky strawberry jam or ½ batch strawberry fruit preserve into the white chocolate ganache after beating the mixture. You could add a few drops of pink food colouring to get an authentic strawberry colour.
- **Hazelnut or nut:** Add 60 ml (¼ cup/4½ fl oz) Nutella or nut butter to milk chocolate ganache filling when beating the mixture. Fold in 100 g (⅔ cup/3½ oz) chopped toasted hazelnuts or any other nuts.
- **Orange:** Add 10 ml (2 t) grated orange zest to the melted chocolate and cream mixture.
- **Lemon:** Add 10 ml (2 t) grated lemon zest to the melted chocolate and cream mixture.
- **Coffee:** Add 10 ml (2 t) instant coffee granules mixed with 10 ml (2 t) water to the chocolate and cream before melting.
- **Liqueur:** Add 30 ml (2 T) of your favourite liqueur to the melted chocolate and cream mixture.
- **Peppermint:** Add 5 ml (1 t) peppermint essence or 5 ml (1 t) fresh chopped mint to the melted chocolate and cream mixture.
- **Turkish delight:** Add 5 ml (1 t) rose water to the melted chocolate and cream mixture and fold 10 chopped Turkish delight sweets into the whipped ganache.

Curd filling

This recipe can be used to make lemon, lime, orange or passionfruit curd. It is not overly sweet and therefore makes an ideal filling to combine with a sweet cake. Makes 750 ml (3 cups/27 fl oz).

Adjust the amount of filling by consulting the table in 'Adjusting the recipe' below.

- 170 g (¾ cup/6 oz) salted butter or baking margarine
- 6 large eggs
- 200 g (1 cup/7 oz) white sugar
- 15 ml (1 T) cornflour (cornstarch/Maizena)
- 375 ml (1½ cup/13½ fl oz) lemon, lime, orange or passionfruit juice or passionfruit pulp
- 5 ml (1 t) zest if making citrus curd

1. Assemble your ingredients.
2. Melt the butter in a pot on the stove over low heat.
3. Whisk together the eggs, sugar, cornflour (cornstarch) and the lemon, lime, orange or passionfruit juice or passionfruit pulp and stir it into the melted butter.
4. Stir continuously until a medium thick custard forms. When the mixture starts to bubble, take it off the heat immediately.
5. Pour the curd into a clean bowl and place clingfilm on the surface of the curd so that a skin does not form. Put the curd in a refrigerator to cool.
6. If you want to cool the curd quickly, line a baking tray (sheet) with clingfilm and then pour the curd onto the tray. A thin layer will cool more quickly. Cover the curd with clingfilm and put it in the refrigerator.
7. Spread onto cake layers to sandwich the layers together.

Tip

Curd filling will keep for seven days if kept refrigerated or inside a refrigerated cake. It can also be frozen for up to three months inside a cake or in an airtight container. Add more sugar if you prefer a sweeter curd filling.

Adjusting the recipe

Adjust the basic recipe by the following amounts for differently sized cakes:

Round cake	15 cm (6 in)	17.5 cm (7 in)	20 cm (8 in)	22 cm (9 in)	25 cm (10 in)	30 cm (12 in)
Square cake	12 cm (5 in)	15 cm (6 in)	17.5 cm (7 in)	20 cm (8 in)	22 cm (9 in)	28 cm (11 in)
Recipe amount	½	¾	1	1¼	1½	2

Fruit preserve filling

This soft, fruity filling is ideal for a dessert cake. Preferably pipe an icing circle with buttercream coating around the edges of the cake layers before filling it with fruit preserve. See 'Filling and coating cakes on p. 11'. The quality of the flavour relies on the quality of the fruit used. Makes 375 ml (1½ cups/13½ fl oz).

Adjust the amount of filling by consulting the table in 'Adjusting the Recipe' on p. 134.

- ✓ 225-300 g (1½ cups/½ lb-10¾ oz) chopped fresh, frozen or canned fruit, such as strawberries, cherries, berries, peaches, apricots, apples, pears, oranges, passionfruit pulp, bananas, mangos, etc.
- ✓ 125 ml (½ cup/4½ fl oz) water, fruit juice or drained syrup from canned fruit
- ✓ 30 ml (2 T) cornflour (cornstarch/Maizena)
- ✓ 50 g (¼ cup/1¾ oz) white sugar
- ✓ 30 ml (2 T) water

1. Assemble your ingredients.
2. Heat the chopped fruit and water, fruit juice or drained syrup together in a pot on the stove. Boil the fruit for about 3-5 minutes to soften.
3. Mix the cornflour (cornstarch) and sugar with the 30 ml (2 T) water and stir it into the boiling fruit.
4. Stir for a few seconds until the mixture thickens and looks clear.
5. Put the fruit preserve in the refrigerator until it has cooled.
6. If you want to cool the fruit preserve quickly, line a baking tray (sheet) with clingfilm and then pour the fruit preserve onto the tray. A thin layer will cool more quickly. Cover the surface of the fruit preserve with clingfilm and put it in the refrigerator.
7. Spread onto cake layers to sandwich the layers together.

Tip
Reduce the amount of sugar in the recipe when using fruit juice or drained syrup.

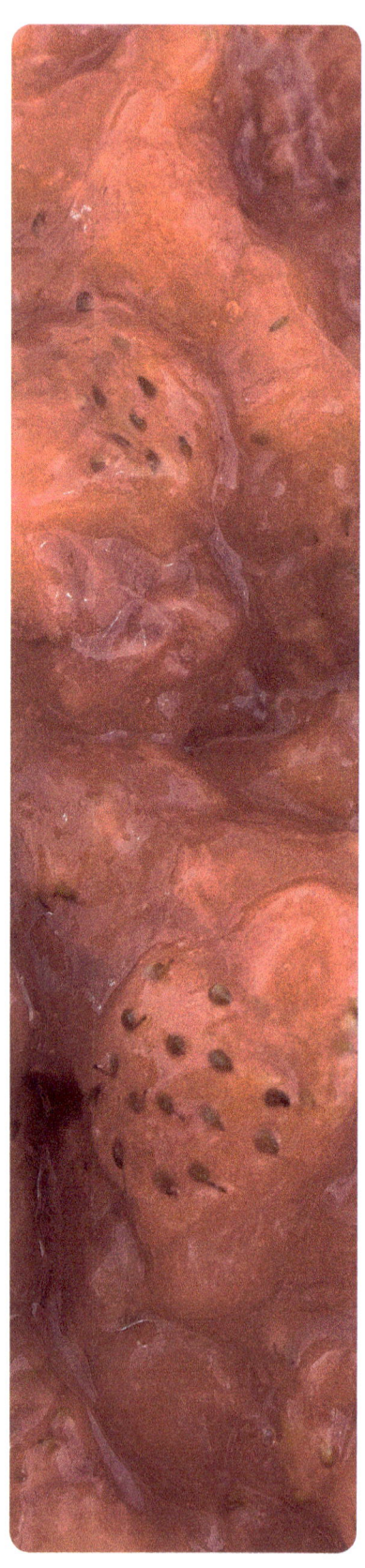

Tip

The filling will keep for up to five days in the refrigerator or inside a refrigerated cake. Fruit preserves do not freeze well.

Adjusting the recipe

Adjust the basic recipe by the following amounts for differently sized cakes:

Round cake	15 cm (6 in)	17.5 cm (7 in)	20 cm (8 in)	22 cm (9 in)	25 cm (10 in)	30 cm (12 in)
Square cake	12 cm (5 in)	15 cm (6 in)	17.5 cm (7 in)	20 cm (8 in)	22 cm (9 in)	28 cm (11 in)
Recipe amount	1	1½	2	2½	3	5

Variations

- **Raspberry:** Keep 30-45 ml (2-3 T) of fresh raspberries separate when making raspberry fruit preserve. Push the finished raspberry preserve through a sieve to remove the seeds and discard. Stir the separate fresh raspberries into the slightly warm mixture.
- **Jam:** If you do not have fresh fruit available, you could use any fruit jam instead. Replace the fruit with the same amount of fruit jam but leave out the white sugar from the recipe.
- **Apple strudel:** Use fresh or canned chopped apple and add the zest and juice of ½ a lemon to the mixture as well as 2.5 ml (½ t) ground cinnamon or mixed spice.

Chocolate mousse filling

This is a rich but light and airy mousse filling. Change the flavour of the mousse according to your dessert theme. The quality of the flavour relies on the quality of the chocolate used. Makes 625 ml (2½ cups/22½ fl oz).

Adjust the amount of filling by consulting the table in 'Adjusting the Recipe' on p. 136

- ✓ 5 ml (1 t) gelatine powder
- ✓ 15 ml (1 T) water
- ✓ 90 g (⅔ cups/3¼ oz) white, milk or dark chocolate
- ✓ 30 g (2 T/1 oz) salted butter or baking margarine
- ✓ 2 large eggs, separated
- ✓ 15 ml (1 T) white sugar
- ✓ 125 ml (½ cup/4½ fl oz) whipping cream
- ✓ 5 ml (1 t) vanilla essence

1. Assemble your ingredients.
2. Sprinkle the gelatine granules over the water and heat the mixture in a microwave for 20-30 seconds to dissolve the gelatine.
3. Melt together the chocolate and butter in a microwave-safe bowl at 20% power or on the defrost setting, stirring at 30-second intervals until the mixture has melted.
4. Stir the melted gelatine into the warm chocolate mixture and set aside to cool slightly.
5. Stir the egg yolks into the cooled chocolate mixture.
6. Beat the egg whites and white sugar with a handheld electric beater or a standing mixer with a whisk attachment until soft peaks form and set aside.
7. Beat the cream and vanilla essence until soft peaks form.
8. Fold the beaten egg whites into the chocolate and egg mixture using a metal spoon or spatula and then fold in the beaten cream.
9. Put the mousse in the refrigerator for 1 hour or longer until it has set.
10. If you want to cool the mousse quickly, line a baking tray (sheet) with clingfilm and then pour the mousse onto the tray. A thin layer will cool more quickly. Cover the mousse with clingfilm and put it in the refrigerator.
11. Spread onto cake layers to sandwich the layers together.

Important: This recipe contains raw eggs and fresh cream; do not serve it to elderly people, small children or pregnant women. Do not leave mousse or a cake filled with mousse out of the refrigerator for longer than 4 hours.

Tip

The chocolate mousse filling will keep for up to three days in the refrigerator or inside a refrigerated cake or two weeks inside a frozen cake. The mousse can also be frozen for up to two weeks in an airtight container but do not add any fruit if you want to freeze the mousse as it will release water when defrosting.

Adjusting the recipe

Adjust the basic recipe by the following amounts for differently sized cakes:

Round cake	15 cm (6 in)	17.5 cm (7 in)	20 cm (8 in)	22 cm (9 in)	25 cm (10 in)	30 cm (12 in)
Square cake	12 cm (5 in)	15 cm (6 in)	17.5 cm (7 in)	20 cm (8 in)	22 cm (9 in)	28 cm (11 in)
Recipe amount	¾	1	1¼	1½	1¾	2½

Variations

- **Fruit:** Fold ½ a batch fruit preserve (p. 133) into a white chocolate mousse mixture after folding in the cream and vanilla.
- **Cheesecake:** Whisk 125 g (½ cup/4½ oz) cream cheese into the cream and vanilla mixture before folding it into the chocolate and egg mixture.
- **Coffee:** Stir 10 ml (2 t) instant coffee granules into the water before sprinkling the gelatine over the water.
- **Liqueur:** Add 45 ml (3 T) liqueur to the chocolate and egg mixture before folding in the cream and vanilla.

Condensed milk custard filling

This easy custard filling is ideal to use between cake layers as it is firm enough to hold up on its own. Flavour this custard to complement your cake. Makes 750 ml (3 cups/27 fl oz).

Adjust the amount of filling by consulting the table in 'Adjusting the recipe' on page 138

- ✓ 500 ml (2 cups/18 fl oz) full cream milk
- ✓ 30 ml (2 T) salted butter or baking margarine
- ✓ 385 g (13¾ oz) can of sweetened condensed milk
- ✓ 1 large egg
- ✓ 45 ml (3 T) cornflour (cornstarch/Maizena)
- ✓ 5 ml (1 t) vanilla essence

1. Assemble your ingredients.
2. Heat together the milk, butter and condensed milk in a pot on the stove at medium heat until the butter has melted.
3. Whisk the egg, cornflour and vanilla essence in a bowl and while whisking, pour some of the heated milk mixture onto the egg mixture.
4. Pour the milk and egg mixture back into the pot and heat it on medium heat on the stove while stirring continuously for about 3 minutes, or until the mixture thickens.
5. As soon as the mixture starts to boil, remove from the heat.
6. Pour the thickened mixture into a bowl, place clingfilm over the surface to prevent a skin forming and put it in the refrigerator until cool.
7. If you want to cool the custard quickly, line a baking tray (sheet) with clingfilm and then pour the cooked custard onto the tray. A thin layer will cool more quickly. Cover the custard with clingfilm and put it in the refrigerator.
8. Spread onto cake layers.

Tip

Condensed milk custard filling will keep for four days in the refrigerator or inside a refrigerated cake or for up to three months inside a frozen cake. The custard can also be frozen for up to three months in an airtight container.

Variations

- **Milk tart:** Add a cinnamon stick to the milk before heating the mixture. Remove it from the thickened custard mixture before refrigerating it. After filling each cake layer, sprinkle powdered cinnamon over the milk tart custard before placing the next layer on top.
- **Traditional:** Replace the 45 ml (3 T) cornflour with 60 ml (¼ cup/2¼ fl oz) instant custard powder.
- **Tea:** Replace 250 ml (1 cup/9 fl oz) of the milk with strongly brewed milky tea.
- **Coffee:** Add 15 ml (1 T) instant coffee powder to the cornflour before heating the mixture or replace 250 ml (1 cup/9 fl oz) of milk with milky coffee.
- **Chocolate:** Add 45 ml (3 T) unsweetened cocoa powder to the cornflour before heating the mixture.
- **Caramel:** Replace the sweetened condensed milk with caramel condensed milk or put the sweetened condensed milk into a large microwave-safe bowl so that the mixture does not boil over and heat in the microwave on high heat stirring at 1-minute intervals for 7 minutes and then stirring at 30-second intervals for about 5 minutes until the condensed milk looks golden brown and caramelized.
- **Coconut:** Replace all or some of the milk with coconut milk and fold 40 g (½ cup/1½ oz) toasted unsweetened desiccated coconut into the finished custard. Replace the vanilla essence with coconut essence if preferred.

Adjusting the recipe

Adjust the basic recipe by the following amounts for differently sized cakes:

Round cake	15 cm (6 in)	17.5 cm (7 in)	20 cm (8 in)	22 cm (9 in)	25 cm (10 in)	30 cm (12 in)
Square cake	12 cm (5 in)	15 cm (6 in)	17.5 cm (7 in)	20 cm (8 in)	22 cm (9 in)	28 cm (11 in)
Recipe amount	½	¾	1	1¼	1½	2

Traditional custard filling

This is my late grandmother's recipe; we still use it for our yearly trifle at Christmas. This custard filling is ideal to use between cake layers as it is firm enough to hold up on its own. Flavour this custard to complement the cake. Makes 750 ml (3 cups/27 fl oz).

Adjust the amount of filling by consulting the table in 'Adjusting the recipe' on p. 140

- ✓ 30 g (¼ cup/1 oz) instant custard powder
- ✓ 50 g (¼ cup/1¾ oz) white sugar
- ✓ 2 large eggs
- ✓ A pinch of salt
- ✓ 500 ml (2 cups/18 fl oz) full cream milk
- ✓ 250 ml (1 cup/9 fl oz) water
- ✓ 5 ml (1 t) vanilla or almond essence or the seeds of 1 vanilla pod

1. Assemble your ingredients.
2. Stir the custard powder and sugar together in a bowl and whisk in the eggs and salt with a balloon whisk.
3. Heat the milk and water in a pot on the stove over medium heat. Remove the pot just before the liquid reaches boiling point.
4. Slowly pour the hot milk mixture over the egg mixture while whisking constantly.
5. Pour the mixture back into the pot and stir over medium heat until the custard thickens and comes almost to a boil.
6. Remove the custard from the heat and stir in the vanilla or almond essence or the seeds of 1 vanilla pod.
7. Pour the thickened mixture into a bowl, place clingfilm over the surface to prevent a skin forming and put it in the refrigerator until cool.
8. If you want to cool the custard quickly, line a baking tray (sheet) with clingfilm and then pour the cooked custard onto the tray. A thin layer will cool more quickly. Cover the custard with clingfilm and put it in the refrigerator.
9. Spread onto cake layers.

Tip

Traditional custard filling will keep for four days in the refrigerator or inside a refrigerated cake. Traditional custard does not freeze well.

Variations

- **Caramel:** Stir together 45 g (¼ cup/1½ oz) brown treacle sugar or demerara sugar, 150 g (½ cup/5 ¼ oz) golden syrup and 60 g (¼ cup/2 oz) salted butter in a pot on the stove at medium heat. Make sure that all the sugar has dissolved and bring to the boil. Boil for about 1-2 minutes. Add 125 ml (½ cup/4½ fl oz) cream and boil for another 2 minutes stirring constantly. Add the caramel sauce to the cooked custard.
- **Coffee:** Add 15 ml (1 T) coffee powder to the custard powder and sugar before whisking in the egg.
- **Lemon or orange:** Add the zest of 1 lemon or 1 orange to the cooked custard mixture.
- **Chocolate:** Add 45 ml (3 T) unsweetened cocoa powder to the custard powder and sugar before whisking in the egg.
- **Tea:** Replace the 250 ml (1 cup/9 fl oz) water with strong brewed milky tea.
- **Coconut:** Replace the 250 ml (1 cup/9 fl oz) water with coconut milk and fold 40 g (½ cup/1½ oz) toasted unsweetened desiccated coconut into the finished custard and replace the vanilla essence with coconut essence if preferred.

Adjusting the recipe

Adjust the basic recipe by the following amounts for differently sized cakes:

Round cake	15 cm (6 in)	17.5 cm (7 in)	20 cm (8 in)	22 cm (9 in)	25 cm (10 in)	30 cm (12 in)
Square cake	12 cm (5 in)	15 cm (6 in)	17.5 cm (7 in)	20 cm (8 in)	22 cm (9 in)	28 cm (11 in)
Recipe amount	½	¾	1	1¼	1½	2

Uncooked caramel filling

This traditional South African caramel filling for caramel peppermint tart is decadently sweet. Preferably create a dam with buttercream coating around the edges of the cake layers before filling it with uncooked caramel. Makes 750 ml (3 cups/27 fl oz)

Adjust the amount of filling by consulting the table in 'Adjusting the recipe' below.

- ✓ 125 ml (½ cup/4½ fl oz) milk
- ✓ 15 ml (1 T) gelatine powder
- ✓ 385 g (13¾ oz) can of caramel condensed milk
- ✓ 250 ml (1 cup/9 fl oz) whipping cream

1. Assemble your ingredients.
2. Sprinkle the gelatine granules over the milk and heat the mixture in a microwave oven on full power for 40-60 seconds or until the gelatine granules have dissolved. Do not let the mixture boil, otherwise the gelatine will not set. Set aside to cool almost to room temperature.
3. Pour the caramel condensed milk and the cream into two separate bowls.
4. Beat the cream until soft peaks form. Do not overbeat as it could split.
5. Add the cooled milk and gelatine mixture to the caramel condensed milk and beat until it looks smooth.
6. Fold the beaten cream into the caramel mixture; the mixture will be quite runny.
7. Put the caramel filling in the refrigerator until cold and thickened.
8. If you want the caramel to set quickly, line a baking tray (sheet) with clingfilm and then pour the caramel onto the tray. A thin layer will cool more quickly. Cover the caramel with clingfilm and put it in the refrigerator.
9. Spread onto cake layers.

Adjusting the recipe

Adjust the basic recipe by the following amounts for differently sized cakes:

Round cake	15 cm (6 in)	17.5 cm (7 in)	20 cm (8 in)	22 cm (9 in)	25 cm (10 in)	30 cm (12 in)
Square cake	12 cm (5 in)	15 cm (6 in)	17.5 cm (7 in)	20 cm (8 in)	22 cm (9 in)	28 cm (11 in)
Recipe amount	½	¾	1	1¼	1½	2

Tip

This caramel filling will keep for four days in the refrigerator or inside a refrigerated cake or frozen for up to two months in a cake.

Lemon condensed milk filling

This traditional South African filling for lemon meringue tart is sweet and tangy. Preferably pipe a circle with buttercream or ganache coating around the edges of the cake layers before filling it with lemon condensed milk. Makes 750 ml (3 cups/27 fl oz).

Adjust the amount of filling by consulting the table in 'Adjusting the recipe' below.

- 1x 385 g (13¾ oz) can of sweetened condensed milk
- 125 ml (½ cup/4½ fl oz) milk
- 10 ml (2 t) cornflour (cornstarch/Maizena) mixed into the milk
- 15 ml (1 T) white sugar
- 2 large eggs
- Zest of 1 lemon
- 250 ml (1 cup/9 fl oz) lemon juice (about 6-8 large lemons)
- 5 ml (1 t) fine table salt

1. Assemble your ingredients.
2. Pour the sweetened condensed milk into a microwave-safe bowl, add the milk and cornflour mixture and the white sugar. Whisk the eggs into the condensed milk with a balloon whisk or fork.
3. Add the lemon zest, lemon juice and salt and stir to incorporate.
4. Microwave the mixture on high for 10 minutes, stirring at 1 to 2-minute intervals until the mixture has thickened.
5. Place clingfilm on the surface of the mixture and then put the lemon condensed milk filling in the refrigerator until cold.
6. If you want the filling to set quickly, line a baking tray (sheet) with clingfilm and then pour the lemon condensed milk onto the tray. A thin layer will cool more quickly. Cover the lemon condensed milk with clingfilm and put it in the refrigerator.
7. Spread onto cake layers.

Adjusting the recipe

Adjust the basic recipe by the following amounts for differently sized cakes:

Round cake	15 cm (6 in)	17.5 cm (7 in)	20 cm (8 in)	22 cm (9 in)	25 cm (10 in)	30 cm (12 in)
Square cake	12 cm (5 in)	15 cm (6 in)	17.5 cm (7 in)	20 cm (8 in)	22 cm (9 in)	28 cm (11 in)
Recipe amount	½	¾	1	1¼	1½	2

Tip

Lemon condensed milk filling will keep for four days in the refrigerator or inside a refrigerated cake or frozen for up to two months inside a cake or an airtight container.

Salted caramel ganache

This ganache has a butterscotch-caramel taste and can be used instead of caramel condensed milk or dulce de leche. It sets medium firm and can be used as a filling or coating. Makes 750 ml (3 cups/27 fl oz).

Adjust the amount of filling by consulting the table in 'Adjusting the recipe' below

- ✓ 80 g (⅓ cup/3 oz) salted butter or baking margarine
- ✓ 160 ml (⅔ cup/6 fl oz) thin cream
- ✓ 60 g (⅓ cup/2¼ oz) dark brown sugar
- ✓ 15 ml (1 T) golden syrup or sweet molasses or treacle syrup
- ✓ 2.5 ml (½ t) fine table salt
- ✓ 400 g (3 cups/14 oz) white chocolate, chopped

1. Heat the butter, cream, brown sugar, golden syrup and salt together in a pot on the stove at a low heat setting and stir until all the sugar has dissolved and the mixture is smooth.
2. Remove the pot from the heat and add the chopped white chocolate to the mixture. Stir until the chocolate has melted and the mixture is smooth.
3. If you want to use the mixture as a filling, pour the ganache into a clean bowl and put in the refrigerator until very cold or preferably overnight.
4. Beat the mixture with a handheld beater until light and fluffy.
5. Spread directly onto the cake layers to sandwich the layers together.
6. If you want to use the mixture as a coating, let it cool down to thicken or leave overnight. If the mixture is too solid, slowly heat again in the microwave oven at 20% power or at the defrost setting at 1-minute intervals and stir until it has softened to a spreadable consistency.
7. Spread directly onto the outside of the cake to cover entirely.

Adjusting the recipe

Adjust the basic recipe by the following amounts for differently sized cakes:

Round cake	15 cm (6 in)	17.5 cm (7 in)	20 cm (8 in)	22 cm (9 in)	25 cm (10 in)	30 cm (12 in)
Square cake	12 cm (5 in)	15 cm (6 in)	17.5 cm (7 in)	20 cm (8 in)	22 cm (9 in)	28 cm (11 in)
Recipe amount	½	¾	1	1¼	1½	2

Tip

The ganache will keep for five days inside a cake at room temperature or refrigerated or for up to two months inside a cake when frozen.

Meringue buttercream filling or coating

It is light and airy and almost like soft marshmallow. The butter gives it a richer flavour and it will enhance the taste of any cake without being overpowering. Makes 750 ml (3 cups/27 fl oz).

Adjust the amount of filling by consulting the table in 'Adjusting the recipe' on p. 145

- ✓ 3 large egg whites
- ✓ 105 g/80 ml (1/3 cup/3¾ oz) liquid glucose (light corn syrup) or golden syrup (buy glucose at your pharmacy)
- ✓ 200 g (1½ cups/7 oz) icing (confectioner's) sugar
- ✓ 5 ml (1 t) vanilla essence or a few drops of vanilla extract
- ✓ 300 g (1⅓ cup/10¾ oz) cool salted butter, cut into small pieces

1. Assemble your ingredients.
2. Put the egg whites, liquid glucose or golden syrup and icing sugar into a bowl that will fit over a pot of simmering water on the stove.
3. Make a double boiler with the bowl suspended over the pot of simmering water, making sure that the stove is set at its lowest setting to keep the water simmering and not boiling and that the water does not touch the bowl. You want the steam from the water to cook the egg mixture.
4. Whisk the egg mixture over the simmering water with an electric beater at medium speed for about 5-7 minutes or until the meringue is light and thick.
5. Remove the bowl from the pot and whisk in the vanilla essence.
6. Put the slightly cooled mixture into the refrigerator for 10-15 minutes to cool down even further. While the mixture is cooling, remove the butter from the refrigerator and cut it into small blocks.
7. Take the mixture out of the refrigerator and beat in the butter a few pieces at a time until all the butter has been incorporated. The meringue might fall flat and become quite liquid, but keep on beating and the mixture will come together and form a fluffy buttercream.
8. If your meringue buttercream remains runny, your added butter may not have been cold enough. Put the bowl into the refrigerator for about 15-30 minutes and beat again until the mixture comes together.

Tip
Meringue buttercream will keep for four days at room temperature inside a cake or in an airtight container and seven days if kept in the refrigerator. It can also be frozen for up to two months. Bring back to room temperature before use.

Variations

- **Coffee:** dissolve 10 ml (2 t) instant coffee granules into 5 ml (1 t) hot water and use it instead of vanilla essence.
- **Berry:** Whisk 60 ml (¼ cup/2¼ fl oz) cooled pureed strawberry, seedless raspberry or cherry fruit preserve (p. 133) or jam into the finished meringue buttercream. Add a few drops of red or purple food colouring to give a more authentic colour.
- **Citrus:** Add the zest of 2 limes, 1 lemon or 1 orange to the finished meringue buttercream and add a few drops of green, yellow or orange food colouring to the mixture. If preferred, whisk a few tablespoons of lime, lemon or orange curd into the buttercream to enhance the flavour but do not add more than 125 ml (½ cup/4½ fl oz) of curd or the meringue buttercream will split.
- **Passionfruit:** Whisk a few tablespoons of passionfruit curd into the buttercream but do not add more than 125 ml (½ cup/4½ fl oz) of curd or the meringue buttercream will split. Add a few drops of yellow food colouring.
- **Coconut:** Fold 40 g (½ cup/1½ oz) toasted unsweetened desiccated coconut into the finished meringue buttercream and replace the vanilla essence with coconut essence.
- **Chocolate:** Add 250 ml (1 cup/9 fl oz) softened (but not hot) chocolate ganache coating to the cooled-down mixture and mix well or dissolve 60 ml (¼ cup/2¼ fl oz) cocoa powder in 60 ml (¼ cup/2¼ fl oz) boiling water. Let it cool and then beat it into the meringue buttercream.
- **Caramel:** Replace the icing sugar with brown treacle sugar and the glucose or light corn syrup with golden syrup. Beat the meringue over the double boiler until all the brown sugar granules have melted and the mixture feels smooth when rubbed between your fingers.
- **7-minute meringue frosting:** Beat the egg white mixture for 5-7 minutes over simmering water. The less time you beat the mixture the softer the meringue will be. If you prefer a thick stiff meringue beat the mixture for a full 7 minutes. Leave out the butter and use the cooled meringue mixture to fill or coat a cake.

Notes:

- If your meringue buttercream looks chunky, your butter might have been too cold when added. Slightly heat the buttercream by blowing hot air onto it with a hairdryer and then whip the buttercream until it looks smooth.
- If your meringue buttercream looks thin and liquid even after beating for quite a while, your butter might have been too warm when it was added or your meringue mixture might still have been too hot when the butter was added. Put the bowl in the refrigerator for 15-30 minutes and beat until the mixture becomes light and fluffy.
- If you have chilled the meringue buttercream and it splits while you re-whip it, put ¼ of the mixture into a bowl and heat in a microwave oven for 10 seconds at a time until it is runny. Beat the runny mixture into the split mixture. This should give you a smooth consistency.

Adjusting the recipe

Adjust the basic recipe by the following amounts for differently sized cakes:

Round cake	15 cm (6 in)	17.5 cm (7 in)	20 cm (8 in)	22 cm (9 in)	25 cm (10 in)	30 cm (12 in)
Square cake	12 cm (5 in)	15 cm (6 in)	17.5 cm (7 in)	20 cm (8 in)	22 cm (9 in)	28 cm (11 in)
Recipe amount	½	¾	1	1¼	1½	2

Traditional buttercream icing

This versatile, rich, sweet and buttery icing can be used as a filling or coating for any type of cake. Makes 750 ml (3 cups/27 fl oz).

Adjust the amount of filling by consulting the table in 'Adjusting the Recipe' below.

- ✓ 230 g (1 cup/8¼ oz) salted butter at room temperature
- ✓ 500 g (4 cups/1 lb 1¾ oz) icing (confectioner's) sugar, sifted
- ✓ 5 ml (1 t) vanilla essence or vanilla extract
- ✓ 15-20 ml (3-4 t) cooled, boiled water
- ✓ Food colouring (optional)

1. Assemble your ingredients.
2. Beat the softened butter and the sifted icing sugar together with a handheld electric beater or a standing mixer on a slow setting. If the icing feels too stiff, add 5 ml (1 t) of cooled, boiled water.
3. Do not beat the icing on a high speed since you do not want to incorporate too many air bubbles.
4. Add the vanilla essence or extract and beat to incorporate.
5. Add food colouring if preferred. If using liquid food colouring, mix it in before adding any water to the buttercream as too much liquid could make the buttercream split.
6. Add a few teaspoons of cooled, boiled water until the icing is at the desired consistency.
7. Place a damp cloth over the bowl or cover the icing with plastic clingfilm so that the surface does not dry out.

Adjusting the recipe

Adjust the basic recipe by the following amounts for differently sized cakes:

Round cake	15 cm (6 in)	17.5 cm (7 in)	20 cm (8 in)	22 cm (9 in)	25 cm (10 in)	30 cm (12 in)
Square cake	12 cm (5 in)	15 cm (6 in)	17.5 cm (7 in)	20 cm (8 in)	22 cm (9 in)	28 cm (11 in)
Recipe amount	½	¾	1	1¼	1½	2

Variations

- **Chocolate:** Dissolve 60 ml (¼ cup/2¼ fl oz) cocoa powder in 60 ml (¼ cup/2¼ fl oz) boiling water. Let it cool and then add it before adding any additional liquid. Add water only if the buttercream feels too stiff.
- **Milk tart:** Add 5 ml (1 t) powdered cinnamon to the buttercream.
- **Hazelnut or nut:** Dissolve 60 ml (¼ cup) cocoa powder in 60 ml (¼ cup) boiling water. Let it cool and then add it to the buttercream before adding any additional water. Also add 125 ml (½ cup/4½ fl oz) Nutella or any nut butter to the buttercream. Add water only if the buttercream feels too stiff.
- **Berry:** Before adding any water, whisk 60 ml (¼ cup/2¼ fl oz) cooled pureed strawberry, seedless raspberry or cherry fruit preserve (p. 133) or fruit jam into the buttercream. Add water only if the buttercream feels too stiff. If preferred, add a few drops of red or purple food colouring.
- **Chocolate Tea:** Steep a tea bag (chai, Earl Grey, English Breakfast or rooibos) in 60 ml (¼ cup/2¼ fl oz) boiling water. Dissolve 60 ml (¼ cup/2¼ fl oz) cocoa powder in the strong black tea. Let it cool and then add it to the buttercream. Add water only if the buttercream feels too stiff.
- **Chai Tea:** Mix 1.25 ml (¼ t) each finely ground cardamom, cinnamon, ginger and nutmeg into the buttercream and add a few teaspoons of cooled brewed tea (any tea) instead of water to the buttercream or mix 60 ml (¼ cup/2¼ fl oz) instant chai tea powder into the buttercream.
- **Caramel:** Make a caramel sauce by stirring together 25 g (2 T/¾ oz) brown treacle sugar or demerara sugar, 75 g (¼ cup/2½ oz) golden syrup and 30 g (2 T/1 oz) salted butter in a pot on the stove at medium heat and bring to the boil making sure that all the sugar has dissolved. Add 60 ml (¼ cup) cream and boil for about 1 minute, stirring constantly. Refrigerate the caramel sauce until very cool. Whisk the caramel sauce into the buttercream before adding any water. Add water to the buttercream only if it feels too stiff.
- **Citrus:** Add the zest of 2 limes, 1 lemon or 1 orange to the finished buttercream and add a few drops of green, yellow or orange food colouring to the mixture. If preferred,, before adding any water to the buttercream, whisk a few tablespoons of lime, lemon or orange curd into the buttercream to enhance the flavour but do not add more than 125 ml (½ cup/4½ fl oz) of curd or the buttercream will split. Add water only if the buttercream feels too stiff.
- **Passionfruit:** Before adding any water, whisk a few tablespoons of passionfruit pulp or curd into the buttercream but do not add more than 125 ml (½ cup/4½ fl oz) of pulp or curd or the buttercream will split. Add a few drops of yellow food colouring. Add water only if the buttercream feels too stiff.
- **Coffee:** Add cooled black coffee to the buttercream icing instead of plain water.
- **White chocolate:** Mix ½ a batch of buttercream with ½ a batch of white chocolate ganache coating at room temperature.
- **Dark chocolate:** Mix ½ a batch of buttercream with ½ a batch of dark chocolate ganache coating at room temperature.
- **Gingerbread:** Mix 5 ml (1 t) ground ginger into the buttercream.
- **Cookies or cake crumb:** Mix 10-15 crushed cookies such as Oreos or 200 g (2 cups/7 oz) cake crumbs into the buttercream.

Tip

Traditional buttercream coating or filling can be kept in an airtight container or inside a cake for five days at room temperature or refrigerated for up to ten days or frozen for three months. Bring back to room temperature before using.

Cream cheese icing

This is a thick icing, ideal to use as a filling for cakes or to pipe on cupcakes. For an authentic cheesecake flavour, add finely grated lemon rind to the mixture. Makes 825 ml (3⅓ cups/29¾ fl oz).

Adjust the amount of filling by consulting the table in 'Adjusting the recipe' below.

- ✓ 600 g (4½ cups/1 lb 5¼ oz) icing (confectioner's) sugar, sifted
- ✓ 150 g (⅔ cup/5¼ oz) salted butter, at room temperature
- ✓ 250 g (1 cup/9 oz) cream cheese, cold from the fridge
- ✓ A few drops of vanilla essence, lemon extract or grated lemon rind

1. Assemble your ingredients.
2. Beat the sifted icing sugar and butter together on a slow speed with a handheld electric beater or a standing mixer until it resembles fine breadcrumbs.
3. Add all the cream cheese and mix for about 2 minutes until light and fluffy. Do not overbeat since this could thin the icing.
4. Add a few drops of vanilla essence, lemon extract or grated lemon rind.
5. If you find the icing too sweet, you could add 5 ml (1 t) of salt and 5 ml ((1 t) of lemon juice to the icing mixture.

Tip

This icing can be stored in an airtight container or inside a cake in the refrigerator for up to four days, or frozen for up to two months. When used as a filling, serve within a few hours or keep the cake refrigerated and bring back to room temperature before use.

Adjusting the recipe

Adjust the basic recipe by the following amounts for differently sized cakes:

Round cake	15 cm (6 in)	17.5 cm (7 in)	20 cm (8 in)	22 cm (9 in)	25 cm (10 in)	30 cm (12 in)
Square cake	12 cm (5 in)	15 cm (6 in)	17.5 cm (7 in)	20 cm (8 in)	22 cm (9 in)	28 cm (11 in)
Recipe amount	½	¾	1	1¼	1½	2

Variations

- **Mascarpone:** Replace all or half of the cream cheese with mascarpone cheese.
- **Pineapple:** Fold 5 ml (1 t) lemon zest and 125 g (½ cup/4½ oz) canned crushed or finely diced pineapple pieces, drained, into the cream cheese icing.

Chocolate ganache coating

Ganache coating sets fairly hard but is still easy to cut through. It makes an excellent outer coating for a cake, sealing in all the flavour and keeping the cake fresh for longer. Makes 750 ml (3 cups/27 fl oz).

Adjust the amount of filling by consulting the table in 'Adjusting the recipe' below

- ✓ 500 g (3½ cups/1 lb 1¾ oz) dark chocolate, chopped or 625 g (4½ cups/1 lb 6¼ oz) milk chocolate, chopped or 750 g (5¼ cups/1 lb 10¾ oz) white chocolate, chopped
- ✓ 250 ml (1 cup/9 fl oz) thin cream

1. Assemble your ingredients.
2. Heat the chopped chocolate and cream together in a bowl in a microwave oven at 20% power or at the defrost setting. Stir at 2-minute intervals until the mixture is melted and smooth.
3. Place a piece of clingfilm over the surface of the ganache so that it does not form a crust. Let the mixture cool down to thicken or leave overnight. If the mixture is too solid, slowly heat again in the microwave oven at 20% power or at the defrost setting for 1-minute intervals and stir until it has softened to a spreadable consistency.
4. Spread directly on the outside of the cake to cover completely.

Adjusting the recipe

Adjust the basic recipe by the following amounts for differently sized cakes:

Round cake	15 cm (6 in)	17.5 cm (7 in)	20 cm (8 in)	22 cm (9 in)	25 cm (10 in)	30 cm (12 in)
Square cake	12 cm (5 in)	15 cm (6 in)	17.5 cm (7 in)	20 cm (8 in)	22 cm (9 in)	28 cm (11 in)
Recipe amount	¼-½	½-¾	¾-1	1-1¼	1¼-1½	1¾-2

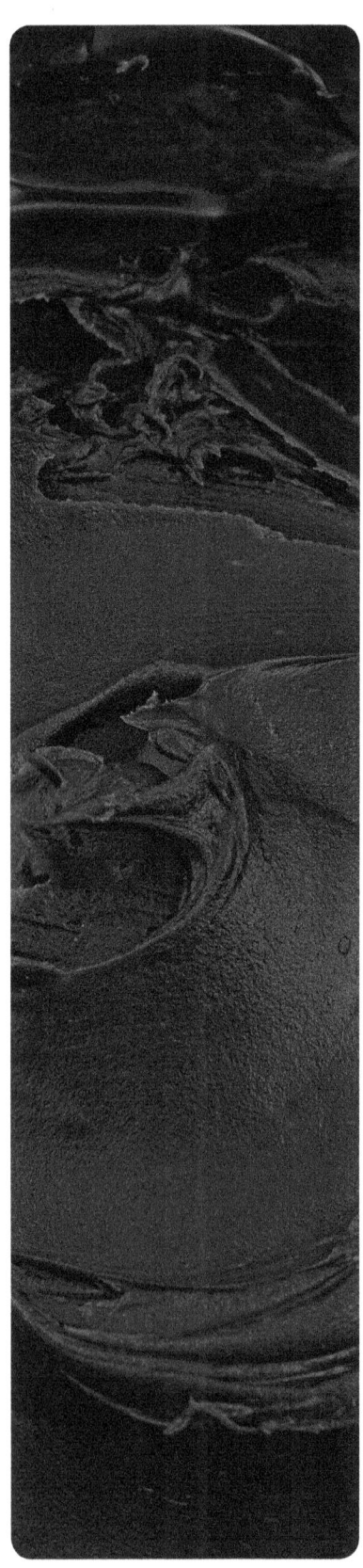

Variations

- **Vanilla:** Add the seeds of 1 vanilla pod to the chocolate and cream before heating.
- **Milk tart:** Use white chocolate and add 5 ml (1 t) cinnamon powder or a cinnamon stick to the cream before heating all together for white chocolate ganache. If you use a cinnamon stick, leave it in the mixture until the ganache has set and then remove the stick before spreading the ganache on the cake.
- **Gingerbread:** Add 5 ml (1 t) ginger powder to the chocolate and cream before heating together.
- **Strawberry:** Use white chocolate and add 5 ml (1 t) strawberry essence and a few drops of pink food colouring to the cream before heating all together for white chocolate ganache coating.
- **Hazelnut- or nut-butter ganache coating:** Add 60 ml (¼ cup/4½ fl oz) Nutella or nut butter to milk chocolate and cream before heating together.
- **Orange:** Add 5 ml (1 t) grated orange zest to dark chocolate and cream before heating together.
- **Lemon:** Add 5 ml (1 t) grated lemon zest to white chocolate and cream before heating together.
- **Coffee:** Add 10 ml (2 t) instant coffee granules mixed with 10 ml (2 t) water to the chocolate and cream before melting.
- **Liqueur:** Add 30 ml (2 T) of your favourite liqueur to the melted chocolate and cream mixture.

Note: If your ganache has overheated, it will separate. Let the ganache cool down and come to almost room temperature, then quickly whip the expelled fat back into the chocolate mixture with a handheld whisk or electric beater until it has been incorporated. Leave the ganache to set and use normally. Experiment with different ratios of chocolate to cream until you find the consistency that works best for you.

Tip

The coating can be refrigerated in an airtight container for up to two months or frozen for six months. Bring back to room temperature before use.

Chocolate glaze

This excellent shiny outer coating sets firmly but is still easy to cut through. Chocolate glaze is heated to just above body temperature or until it is thin enough to pour over the cake. Makes 560 ml (2¼ cups/20 fl oz) dark, milk or white chocolate glaze

Adjust the amount of glaze by consulting the table in 'Adjusting the recipe' on p. 152

- ✓ 10 ml (2 t) granulated powder gelatine or 2 leaves of gelatine
- ✓ 125 ml (½ cup/4½ fl oz) thin cream
- ✓ 125 ml (½ cup/4½ fl oz) water
- ✓ 30 ml (2 T) liquid glucose (light corn syrup) or golden syrup (buy glucose at your pharmacy)
- ✓ 290 g (2 cups/10¼ oz) dark chocolate, chopped or 370 g (2⅔ cups/13¼ oz) milk or white chocolate, chopped
- ✓ Food colouring (optional)
- ✓ 5 ml (1 t) flavouring essence (optional)

1. Assemble your ingredients.
2. Sprinkle the granulated powder gelatine over 15 ml (1 T) of cold water and leave to sponge or soak the 2 leaves of gelatine in a small amount of water.
3. Heat the cream, water and liquid glucose or golden syrup in a microwave oven at full power, stirring at 1-minute intervals until the mixture is very hot and almost boiling.
4. Stir the bloomed gelatine into the hot cream mixture.
5. Add the chopped dark, milk or white chocolate to the hot cream mixture and stir the mixture until the chocolate has melted and the mixture is smooth.
6. If the mixture starts to cool and all the chocolate has not melted, put it back in the microwave oven and heat at full power, stirring at 30-second intervals until the chocolate has melted and the mixture feels smooth.
7. If preferred, add a few drops of food colouring and 5 ml (1 t) flavouring essence to the glaze.
8. Refrigerate the mixture for 15-30 minutes or more to cool and thicken slightly or cover the surface of the mixture with clingfilm and let it stand to thicken overnight at room temperature or in the refrigerator.
9. Reheat the chocolate glaze in a microwave oven at full power, stirring at 30-second intervals until it is runny enough to pour over the cake. It should have the consistency of thin custard. The glaze should be only slightly warmer than body temperature. Do not overheat, otherwise it will melt your coating underneath.

Tip

- A white chocolate glaze can be coloured with food colouring.
- A cake covered with chocolate glaze can be kept for a few days at room temperature or stored in an airtight container in the refrigerator.
- The chocolate glaze can be refrigerated in an airtight container for up to one month or frozen for six months. Bring back to room temperature before use.

10. Place a slightly chilled ganache- or buttercream-coated cake on a cooling rack over a baking tray (sheet) and pour the glaze over the cake, preferably through a sieve to burst air bubbles and catch any particles such as unmelted chocolate pieces, completely covering the sides and moving the sieve and glaze towards the middle of the cake to cover the top of the cake.

11. Scrape the glaze from the baking tray and pour onto any part of the cake that was not covered the first time. Pour leftover glaze into a container to reuse for another cake.

12. Put the cake, still on the cooling rack or placed on a serving plate, into the refrigerator for 20-30 minutes for the glaze to set.

Adjusting the recipe

Adjust the basic recipe by the following amounts for differently sized cakes:

Round cake	15 cm (6 in)	17.5 cm (7 in)	20 cm (8 in)	22 cm (9 in)	25 cm (10 in)	30 cm (12 in)
Square cake	12 cm (5 in)	15 cm (6 in)	17.5 cm (7 in)	20 cm (8 in)	22 cm (9 in)	28 cm (11 in)
Recipe amount	½	¾	1	1¼	1½	2½

Notes:
- If you see any air bubbles on top of the glaze, you can blow over it with a hairdryer to burst the bubbles.
- If you see any air bubbles on the glaze after pouring it on the cake, quickly burst it with a pin before it starts to set.
- You will always have glaze left over since the poured glaze will drip off the cake. Keep the leftover glaze for another project, or use as glue to stick decorations to a glaze-covered cake. Dip the tops of cupcakes, éclairs or profiteroles into the glaze or eat as a sauce with ice cream.

Meringues

These meringues are light and crunchy and very sweet. Use them whole as decoration on a cake or crushed inside. Makes 20-25 medium-sized or 120-140 mini meringues or a 20 cm (8 in) meringue disc or 8-10 mini meringue discs (7.5 cm/3 in).

- ✓ 60 g (2 oz) or 2 large egg whites, at room temperature
- ✓ a pinch of cream of tartar or 2 drops of lemon juice
- ✓ 105 g (½ cup/3¾ oz) castor sugar
- ✓ 2.5 ml (½ t) vanilla essence
- ✓ A few drops of food colouring (optional)

1. Preheat the oven to 120 °C (250 °F) for a conventional oven or 100 °C (215 °F) for a fan-assisted oven.
2. Line a baking tray (sheet) with non-stick baking paper and spray it with non-stick cooking spray.
3. Put the egg whites in a clean, dry bowl and beat at a slow speed with a handheld electric beater or a standing mixer with whisk attachment. When starting to beat the egg whites, they will have a light hue and will look translucent and large foam bubbles will form, but as you keep on beating, the mixture will become whiter with finer foam bubbles.
4. When the egg whites look frothy, add the cream of tartar or 2 drops of lemon juice.
5. Beat the egg whites at medium speed to the soft peak stage: when you lift your beaters out of the egg whites, a soft point will form that falls back on itself.
6. Beat the castor sugar into the egg whites, about one teaspoon at a time, beating continuously until all the sugar has dissolved before adding more sugar.
7. By the time the last sugar is added, the egg whites should form stiff peaks. If not, continue beating the mixture. When the beaters are lifted out of the meringue mixture, a firm point should form that does not fall back on itself.
8. Add the vanilla essence and optional food colouring to the meringue and fold it in.
9. To make marbled meringues, fold in a few drops of food colouring such as yellow and orange so that the mixture is slightly marbled. Stop folding in the

food colouring when you see streaks of colour here and there but can still see some white mixture.

10. To make medium-sized meringues, use 2 teaspoons to scoop the meringue out of the bowl. Scoop with one spoon and scrape off the mixture onto the lined baking tray with the other spoon.
11. To make spiky meringues, use one of the spoons or a fork to create points and peaks on each meringue by touching the spoon or fork onto the surface of the meringue and quickly lifting it away again.
12. Put the baking tray into the oven and immediately turn down the oven to 100 °C (215 °F) for a conventional oven or 90 °C (195 °F) for a fan-assisted oven.
13. Bake medium-sized meringues for 1 hour and 30 minutes and then turn off the oven and leave the meringues in the oven until it is cool.

To make mini meringues

1. Line 2 baking trays with non-stick baking paper.
2. Cut a small hole of about 1 cm (½ in) into the tip of a large zip-lock bag or a disposable piping bag or use a 1 cm (½ in) piping nozzle inside the bag. Spoon the meringue mixture into the bag and pipe small blobs of the mixture onto the trays.
3. Bake mini meringues for 35-45 minutes.

Tip

Meringues, mini meringues, a meringue disc or mini meringue discs will keep for two weeks in airtight containers at room temperature or can also be frozen for up to three months.

To make a meringue disc

 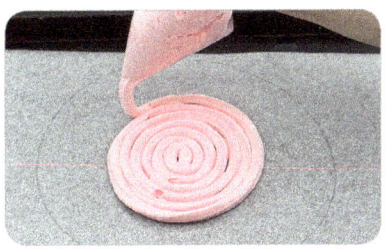 

1. Line a baking tray with non-stick baking paper and use a 20 cm (8 in) cake tin to draw a circle on the back of the paper. Spray the front with non-stick cooking spray.
2. Spoon the meringue mixture into a large zip-lock bag or disposable piping bag and cut off the tip of the bag to create a 1 cm (½ in) hole.
3. Pipe a meringue spiral on the drawn circle starting in the middle and moving the bag outwards until the whole circle has been filled or fill the whole circle with piped meringues starting on the outside edge of the circle and moving inwards.
4. If you prefer not to pipe the meringue mixture, just spread it evenly on the circle with a palette knife.
5. Bake the meringue disc at 120 °C (250 °F) for a conventional oven or 100 °C (215 °F) for a fan-assisted oven for 1 hour and then turn the oven down to 100 °C (215 °F) for a conventional oven or 90 °C (195 °F) for a fan-assisted oven and bake for 1 more hour.
6. Turn off the oven and leave the meringue disc in the oven until it is cool.

To make mini meringue discs

1. Line a baking tray with non-stick baking paper and use a round object such as a glass of 7.5 cm (3 in) wide to draw circles on the back of the paper. Spray the front with non-stick cooking spray.
2. Pipe meringue spirals on the drawn circles starting in the middle of each circle and moving the bag outwards until each circle is filled or spread the meringue mixture evenly on the circles with a palette knife.
3. Bake the mini meringue discs at 120 °C (250 °F) for a conventional oven or 100 °C (215 °F) for a fan-assisted oven for 30 minutes and then turn the oven down to 100 °C (215 °F) for a conventional oven or 90 °C (195 °F) for a fan-assisted oven and bake for another 1 hour.
4. Turn off the oven and leave the mini meringue discs in the oven until the oven is cool.

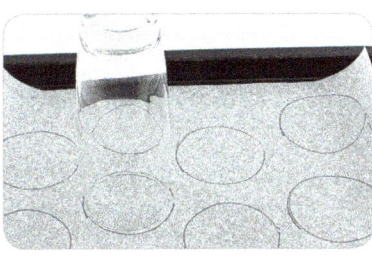

French macarons

French macarons have a crunchy shell and a chewy centre and are very sweet. Fill them with ganache, buttercream, jam or any other filling. I have not given volume amounts for the ingredients as everything has to be weighed precisely. Makes 50 single macarons or 25 sandwiched macarons of 3.5 cm (1⅓ in) in diameter or 160 single mini macarons or 80 sandwiched mini macarons of 2.5 cm (1 in) in diameter.

- 100 g (3½ oz) icing (confectioner's) sugar
- 25 g (1 oz) cornflour (cornstarch) or cocoa powder
- 50 g (1¾ oz) ground, flaked or slivered almonds
- 60 g (2 oz) or 2 large egg whites, at room temperature
- 65 g (2¼ oz) white castor (granulated) sugar
- 2.5 ml (½ t) almond or vanilla essence
- Liquid, gel or powder food colouring
- 5 ml (1 t) filling per standard sandwiched macaron or 1.25 ml (¼ t) filling per mini sandwiched macaron or 125 ml (½ cup/4½ fl oz) of filling for the full macaron recipe, such as buttercream, ganache or jam

1. Preheat your conventional oven to 160 °C (325 °F).

   Note: I prefer to bake standard macarons at 150 °C (300 °F) for 15 minutes or mini macarons at 130 °C (270 °F) for 15-18 minutes (lower heat and slower cooking time) but you will have to test a few batches in your oven to get the perfect temperature and baking time for yours. I measure with a separate oven thermometer placed inside my oven.

2. The macarons are baked on the back of two baking trays (sheets) fitting into each other. Ideally you need 4 trays of equal size so that you can prepare one set while the other is baking, but if you have only one set, you can reuse it later after baking your first batch of macarons.

3. Cut 2 sheets of non-stick baking paper to fit on the backs of your two sets of baking trays. Prepare templates for the standard macarons by drawing 25 x 3.5 cm (1⅓ in) circles on the back of each paper sheet with a pencil, using a round object such as the wide end of a piping nozzle. You could also print circles on a piece of paper to put underneath your non-stick baking paper. Make the macarons as small or large as you prefer.

4. Place 2 baking trays upside-down on top of one another on a folded dishcloth on your counter and place a prepared non-stick baking paper sheet and template on top, with the pencil marks towards the trays so that they do not transfer onto the macarons.

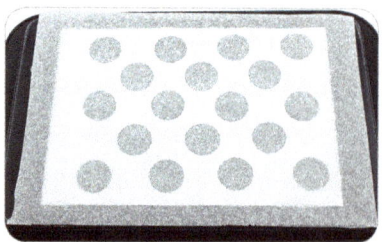 

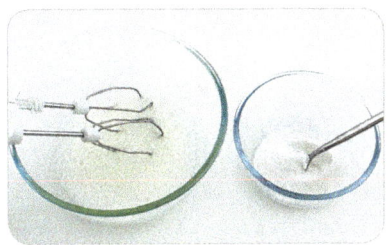

5. Assemble your ingredients. Pulse the icing sugar, cornflour or cocoa powder and ground, flaked or slivered almonds together in a food processor or with the processing attachment of an immersion blender until it looks like fine breadcrumbs. (If you blend the mixture too long it will form lumps. If this happens, sift the mixture. Pulse any large almond pieces that have stayed behind in the sieve and pour back into the mixture.) Set aside.

6. Put the egg whites in a clean, dry bowl and beat with a handheld electric beater on slow to medium speed or a standing mixer with whisk attachment on slow speed. When starting to beat the egg whites, they will have a light yellow hue and will look translucent and large foam bubbles will form, but as you keep on beating, the mixture will become whiter with finer foam bubbles. Beat the egg whites to the soft peak stage: when you lift your beaters out of the egg whites a soft point will form that falls back on itself.

7. Add the castor sugar to the egg whites a teaspoonful at a time while beating continuously at medium speed until a firm meringue is formed. By the time the last sugar is added, the egg whites should form stiff peaks. When the beaters are lifted out of the meringue mixture, a firm point should form that does not fall back on itself.

8. Fold the almond or vanilla essence and a few drops of liquid or gel food colouring into the egg whites. If you want separate colours, divide the mixture and then stir in food colouring. Too much food colouring will change the consistency of the mixture; therefore if you want very dark macarons, rather use powder food colouring.

9. Fold the almond mixture into the egg whites with a spatula in two batches, until no more dry ingredients are visible and the mixture looks fully blended together. Give 20 or more folds until the mixture feels softer, but not runny. When you lift your spatula out of the mixture, a soft point will form that falls back on itself.

10. Cut a small hole of about 1 cm (½ in) into one corner of a large zip-lock bag or into the tip of a disposable piping bag or use a 1 cm (½ in) piping nozzle inside the bag. (A small hole will help to burst unwanted air bubbles in the mixture.) Spoon the macaron mixture into the bag.

11. Stick the prepared baking paper to the trays by piping a dot of macaron mixture underneath each side of the paper so that the paper lies flat.

12. Pipe small rounds of macaron mixture following the drawn or printed circles.

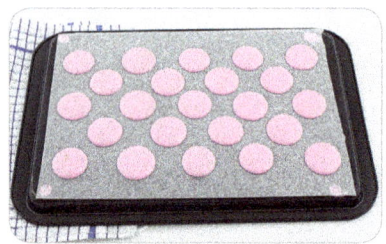

13. Each time after piping 8-10 macarons, tap the baking trays a few times on a folded dishcloth on your workbench until the macarons flatten out and no points are visible. If you have tapped the trays a few times and the points on the macarons are still visible, your mixture might be too stiff. Pipe all of the mixture back into the bowl and then spoon it back into your piping bag. This will help loosen it.

14. As soon as you have finished piping macarons on one set of baking trays, place the double set of trays lengthways in the centre of your oven on the middle oven rack. Turn down the oven to 150 °C (300 °F) and bake the standard macarons for 14-16 minutes. (If you only have one set of baking trays, leave them to cool for 5-10 minutes after baking and reuse them for the rest of the macarons.)

15. Finish piping the second batch of macarons, remembering to tap the trays every now and again. (It does not matter that these macarons will be sitting for a while before being baked.)

16. When the first batch is done, take the macarons out of the oven and let them sit for a few minutes on the warm trays before lifting off the sheet of baking paper and placing the sheet with macarons on a cool work surface.

17. When the oven has again reached the correct temperature, place the second batch in the oven.

18. Let the macarons cool slightly and then lift them off the non-stick baking paper.

19. Fill the macarons by spooning the filling into a zip-lock bag or disposable piping bag and pipe a dollop of filling onto half of the macarons. Place macarons of equal size on top of the filling, twist and press the macarons lightly to evenly distribute the filling inside. If they are too dry or crispy, leave them uncovered in a refrigerator for 8 hours or overnight to soften.

To make mini macarons

1. Preheat your conventional oven to 140 °C (285 °F).
2. Cut 3 sheets of non-stick baking paper to fit on the back of 3 sets of baking trays. Prepare templates for the mini macarons by drawing 50 x 2.5 cm (1 in) circles on the back of each paper sheet with a pencil using a round object such as the wide end of a small piping nozzle. You could also print circles on a piece of paper to use underneath your non-stick baking paper.
3. Make the macaron mixture as described above and spoon it into a large zip-lock bag or piping bag.
4. Pipe small rounds of macaron mixture following the drawn or printed circles.
5. Place the baking trays lengthways in the centre of your oven on the middle oven rack, turn down the oven temperature to 130 °C (270 °F) and bake mini macarons for 15-18 minutes. (If you only have one set of baking trays leave them to cool for 5-10 minutes after baking and reuse them for the rest of the macarons.)

Tips

- If your macarons stick to the non-stick baking paper, they have not been baked long enough. Put them back into the oven and bake for a few more minutes or turn down the oven temperature to 120 °C (250 °F) and dry them out for 15 minutes as you would meringues.
- To make marbled macarons, add a few drops of food colouring to the finished macaron mixture and swirl it with a toothpick.
- Make sure that your oven temperature stays below or at 160 °C (325 °F) otherwise the macarons might brown too much.
- Do not grease or spray the non-stick baking paper with non-stick cooking spray otherwise the 'foot' will lift up.
- If you have a large enough oven to fit in two sets of baking trays (sheets) next to each other you could pipe the mixture onto two sets of baking trays and put them in the oven simultaneously. If your oven does not bake evenly, turn the trays around after 10-12 minutes so that the macarons bake uniformly.
- Macarons will keep for seven days in an airtight container at room temperature or in the refrigerator. They can also be frozen for 5-6 months. Bring back to room temperature before serving.

Suppliers

SOUTH AFRICA

CAB FOODS
Baking supplies, Orley chocolate, chocolate discs, almond paste (marzipan), fondant icing (sugar paste)
Cape Town Tel: 021 981 6778
sales@cabfoods.co.za

SOUTH BAKELS
Baking supplies, Ready-to-roll Pettinice fondant icing, Choccex cooking chocolate
Cape Town Tel: 021 951 1388
Johannesburg Tel: 011 673 2100
Nelspruit Tel: 013 752 3974
East London Tel: 043 736 2941
Port Elizabeth Tel: 041 399 6600
Bloemfontein Tel: 051 432 8445
www.sbakels.co.za

YUPPIECHEF
Cutters, stencils, small non-stick rolling pins, cake decorating tools, baking equipment, cake cutting wire
www.yuppiechef.com

ELEMENTALS
Food-safe stencils
Cape Town Tel: 021 794 2933
www.elementals.co.za

VALUE BAKING SUPPLIES
Baking supplies, cake decorating equipment, cake cutting wire, baking chocolate, almond paste (marzipan), fondant icing (sugar paste)
Cape Town Tel: 021 981 0304
www.valuesupplies.co.za

CHEFS 'N ICERS
Baking supplies, equipment
Johannesburg Tel: 011 783 3201
www.chefs-n-icers.co.za

THE CHOCOLATE DEN
Baking supplies, chocolate products
Johannesburg Tel: 011 453 8160
www.chocolateden.co.za

USA

WILTON
Baking equipment, candy coating
www.wilton.com

GLOBAL SUGAR ART
Cake decorating equipment
www.globalsugarart.com

UK

SQUIRES SHOP
Baking supplies, cake decorating equipment
www.squires-shop.com

CARINA'S CUPCAKES
Cake decorating equipment, cake smoothers
www.carinascupcakes.co.uk

Sponsors

I would like to thank South Bakels for sponsoring Choccex chocolate (Tel: 011 673 2100, www.sbakels.co.za) as well as Value Baking Supplies for sponsoring consumables (Tel: 021 981 0304, www.valuesupplies.co.za).

www.ingramcontent.com/pod-product-compliance
Lightning Source LLC
Chambersburg PA
CBHW051253110526
44588CB00026B/2984